12 Weeks in Thailand
The Good Life on the Cheap

12 Weeks in Thailand
The Good Life on the Cheap

Johnny FD

2013

Copyright © 2013 Johnny FD

All rights reserved. This book or any portion thereof may not be reproduced or used in any manner whatsoever without the express written permission of the publisher except for the use of brief quotations in a book review or scholarly journal.

First Printing: 2013

ISBN 978-1-300-68566-1

www.12WeeksinThailand.com

Dedication

Thank you to those who have given me the strength and courage to go after what I think will make me happy. To my mother for trying to raise me the best she knew. To my father for working so hard his entire life to give me the freedom to make my own choices. To my sister Christina, for never judging me and always showing me love.

I want to thank Timothy Ferris, the author of the 4-hour workweek, without your book, I never would have had the tools or confidence to move to Thailand on a whim. To my cousins Larry and Jacob for taking me on that first trip, the one that started it all. Michael Galvin for your valuable suggestions on gyms.

Thank you to my blog readers, without you, I'd have no one to write this book for. I know that if a book like this had existed, I would have quit my job and moved to Thailand long ago and not wasted so much precious time and money along the way.

Contents

Chapter 1: Introduction

- My Story and why this book may change your life.

- If you hate your job and dream about coming to Thailand.

Chapter 2: Planning your trip

- The best time to come to Thailand.

- The month to absolutely avoid.

- Responsibilities, bills, and other reasons why you're not here already.

- A list of things you MUST do before you come.

- How to make your three grand last 3 months instead of 3 weeks.

- What to Pack: Things to bring with you to Thailand

- Budgeting and Saving: How much you should expect to spend.

- Costs of living in Phuket vs. Chiang Mai

- Actual spreadsheet of one month's expenses in Koh Tao.

- Living on the islands: Koh Tao, Koh Samui and Koh Lanta.

Chapter 3: Making Money while in Thailand

- Living as a professional fighter off of your fight purse.

- Getting a local job – Tourism, Writer, Teacher or Guide.

- Scooter Empire – Make money renting out bikes.

- Slanging' Seeds – How I paid for my time in Phuket.
- Making money online – Blogs, eBooks and Internet Marketing.
- Online Gigs – How to make a couple bucks here and there.
- Passive income - How to make money online while traveling.

Chapter 4: Life as a Divemaster turned Scuba Instructor

- From Zero to Hero: Taking the leap from newbie to professional in just 3 months.
- Becoming a Scuba Instructor: Why it may kill your passion for diving.
- Combining Scuba Diving and Muay Thai/MMA – Live the dream and get the best of both worlds.
- Girlfriends and Dating: The best places to hook up, long term relationships and why you shouldn't date a Thai girl.
- Climbing Mountains and Learning how to push myself past my limits.
- Living and working on beautiful tropical islands.

Chapter 5: Muay Thai and MMA Training Camps

- Prefight camp homework: Get in shape and be prepared for it.
- What is the best gym in Phuket, Bangkok, Chiang Mai, and Pattaya?
- What is the best Muay Thai Gym in all of Thailand?
- What is the best overall MMA Gym in all of Thailand?
- The worst Muay Thai gym I've ever trained at.
- Getting ripped off for training – Why you might be overpaying.

- Muay Thai and MMA Schools: How to get a discount at every camp and why I've never had to pay more than 5,000 baht a month for training.

- Fighting Muay Thai in Thailand – Everything you want to know.

- How to avoid fighting a Taxi driver that may take a fall on purpose.

- How to Win your First Professional Fight – and why losing it may actually be better in the long run.

- Fighting MMA in Asia – How to get MMA fights in China, Malaysia, Philippines and Thailand.

Chapter 6: Temping things you really should avoid.

- Steroids and HGH – Who uses them, how to get them, and why you shouldn't do them.

- Recreational Drugs – Weed, Ecstasy, Mushrooms, Opium, and Amphetamines, prices, availability, and why I don't touch the stuff.

- Bar girls, Hookers, and Prostitutes: Why normal guys that would never normally pay for sex, end up doing so in Thailand, and why I chose to stay away from them.

Chapter 7: Even more value for your money.

- Practical Information: Doing Laundry and Day to day Life.

- 10 Days of Silent Meditation, living in a Monastery in Thailand. Eat, sleep and meditate like a monk, all on a donation only basis.

- Airfare: How I got my job to pay for my airfare from the U.S. to Thailand

- Tattoos: Where to get authentic bamboo style Thai tattoos done by a monk, for free.

- Exchanging Cash vs. Travelers Checks: Why neither are a great idea.

- Withdrawing from an ATM: How to get all of your ATM Fees refunded.

- Credit Card: How to avoid the unsuspecting 3% international currency exchange fee that will hit you like a brick two months after you get home.

- Restaurant Thai: The 10 or so words I use on a daily basis.

- Basic Polite Thai: The other 10 or so words I know, which get me by in Muay Thai gyms and other random places.

- Special Diets in Thailand: Vegetarian, Vegan, Religious and Paleo

- My biggest fears, and my quest for freedom: Making the plunge into your own 12 weeks in Thailand.

- Contact me: How to ask me anything your inquiring mind may want to know.

Introduction

Chapter 1: Introduction

It took me almost thirty years and traveling half way around the globe to find out what really makes me happy. To figure out who am I, and what am I passionate about?

The heart of it came to me while sitting on top of the ocean, over the clear tropical waters off the coast of Phuket. I had just learned to breathe underwater for my first time, but more importantly how to really be alive. I know it sounds like a lot, but it happened, and I didn't expect it. I was actually quite happy right before I came to Thailand, I had it all, the beautiful blonde girlfriend, a convertible sports car, and access to the hottest nightclubs in Los Angeles. But it turns out, none of that shit really made me happy, it was all a facade.

Diving became my first passion, which lead me to come back to Thailand for 12 more weeks, then I discovered Muay Thai and MMA which made me come back yet again for 12 more. It was a vicious cycle that could not be broken. Every time I could go back to the states, I would think about staying, life there really isn't bad...but then winter comes and even though it's not nearly as cold in California as it is in the rest of the world, I feel the need to escape.

On the sundeck of a dive ship, while eating what may have been the best tasting meal I've ever had, a simple dish of fried chicken and spaghetti, I met a man that forever changed my life. His name was René Christoffersen and he was my scuba diving instructor. The funny thing was, my cousin and I showed up that morning, both absolutely unprepared for what was in store for us. We didn't even think to bring a towel or swim trunks. We ended up walking around in wet underpants the whole day. Yet it ended up being one of the best days of our lives. Imagine that.

Scuba diving was so out of our realm of reality and I had no idea what to expect. The idea of getting wet hadn't even occurred to either of us. To think, so little time has actually passed since taking that first flight, to selling all of my belongings and moving across the world, to throwing my first kick in Muay Thai, and attempting my first submission in MMA, all the way to taking my first fight. Thinking back, it all seemed so magical. But then again, if it was going to happen anywhere, it would happen in Thailand.

My Story and why this book may change your life.

I did what every kid was supposed to do. I got good grades in school, got accepted into a high ranking university, graduated with honors and landed an office job with one of the biggest corporations in America. I even almost married my college sweetheart.

I had always heard of Thailand. People that went all came back ecstatic. It's funny, no one ever comes back from Thailand saying, it was okay. Everyone raves about how amazing it was, I guess that's why they call it, Amazing Thailand.

Even though I knew I wanted to go one day, it seemed like something always came up, either the lack of time or money. Usually both. However this time, I was destined to finally go, but even destiny has it's challengers. About a month before my first trip to Thailand, a huge business opportunity came up and it would have been logical for me to cancel my trip. It was basically a promotion that would have came with more money and recognition within my industry.

To be honest, if it wasn't the fact that I had planned the trip months ago with my two cousins, I would have canceled. It was just bad timing to go and if it was just friends and not family, I probably would have postponed the trip, maybe even indefinitely. Blood really is thicker than water in that sense.

This blood, carried me across the ocean, where I finally made it to Thailand. We flew into Bangkok and proceeded to get a two hour massage, tipping way too much like typical Americans do. I think that we ended up getting a total of 30 massages in 21 days while we were there. Overkill, I know. After breakfast in the mornings we would be the first customers as they were opening, and while walking around, if we were ever bored, we'd just pop in and get a foot massage to kill some time.

It was a combination of mindless spending, knowing that we only had three weeks to enjoy ourselves before going back to reality, and the fact that everything was so damn cheap. For the cost of one massage in the U.S. we could get 10, so why wouldn't we get one everyday?

It was this mentality that made us try to pack in as many things we could into a short amount of time. We flew down to Phuket to see the legendary white sand beaches and tropical blue water first hand. At our hotel, we were the only ones not on honeymoon. We then proceeded to sign up for every tour imaginable.

The first day, was a snorkeling trip to Koh Phi Phi, the island from Leonardo DiCaprio's movie "The Beach" was filmed. We then signed up for a day's worth of Elephant trekking, followed by a Thai Cooking Class, Bungy Jumping, something called Phuket Fantasy which was like a really strange Thai Disneyland type experience. Eventually we ended up signing up for our discover scuba diving class.

That was the beginning to everything. I've always heard about scuba diving from books and on TV, mainly Discovery Channel and BBC Wild, and in movies featuring James Bond. Also, I had absolutely no intention of doing it more than once. I even paid a guy 2,000 baht ($66US) to take pictures of me underwater so I could have proof that I was down there.

This is a photo from the first time I ever went diving. It's funny that something I thought I would only do once, I've ended up doing close to 800 more times since.
If you hate your job and dream about coming to Thailand.

I didn't even realize I hated my job until I met Rene. I thought I was just stressed and needed a vacation. I had read the 4-hour workweek on the plane ride over, but never thought for a second of actually moving to another country, especially not Thailand.
I'm sure Rene got asked these questions all of the time and was sick of answering them. But luckily, I was persistent. If only a book like this existed back then, he could have just pointed me to the website and told me to read it.

"Read 12 Weeks in Thailand, then decide for yourself." He could have said.

Johnny FD

I found a piece of paper and a pen, and disappeared to the front of the ship writing out a list of pros and cons of moving to Thailand and a list of everything holding me back from doing so. I factored in the cost of living, visas, health insurance, everything I could think of. An hour later, I ran back up to Rene who was happily drinking an ice cold beer on the top deck, ecstatic to show him my list and tell him that I've made my decision to move to Thailand. He wasn't as excited as I imagined he'd be, in hindsight I doubt he believed me, as I'm sure exactly 20% of his students say the same thing and none of them actually go through with it.
Well, I guess I was the exception I wrote the following letter to my business partner and roommate at the time, setting it all in stone, planting the seed that would sprout into a forest, one that couldn't be undone.

Here's the actual letter that I wrote, setting it all in motion.

Written: Oct 22, 2008

Subject: Private Letter to JT (important and confidential),

JT,

This last year and a half has been an amazing journey.
 I think that us meeting has been fate, and we've mutually complimented each other so well in our strong suits to balance each other out. We're both at a much better place than we were before we met, our careers, community standing, and lives.

We have both tremendously helped each other in uncountable ways. When you said to me the other week, "Johnny, thank you, I couldn't have done it without you." That meant a lot to me. And I want to tell you that I couldn't have done it without you either.
 But internally, I'm burnt out.

 I want to step down from helping you run the company as your Vice President. For the last 18 months, I've been doing a tremendous workload, a lot of which goes unseen. Life feels too hectic and I feel like I'm wearing 30 different hats and I don't have time to dedicate myself to any of the roles to its fullest potential.

I don't know what I want, I don't know where life is taking me, but I know that I haven't been happy.

It wasn't until last week when I jumped into the ocean, having no idea what was in store for me, scuba gear in place, and breathing apparatus in mouth, did I really open my eyes and feel stress free for the first time in a very long time. Maybe its the idea of not being able to talk, finally, or really concentrating on my breathing....maybe its the clear water and beautiful ocean life. Maybe its the feeling of being weightless, and discovering a new world. But whatever it is, I was happy.

Since then, I've been scuba diving four more times, and have taken classes and quizzes to work towards my scuba diving certification. I am now officially PADI Open Water Certified. I'd hope you'd be happy and proud of me.

However, I don't expect anyone to understand, so I'm not going to tell many people until I'm gone. But I've decided that I am moving to a small island called Koh Tao, Turtle Island. Life is simple there, no nightclubs, traffic, or stress. Life is hiking in the jungle, running on the white sand beaches, and diving in the clear waters. I'm going to pursue the rest of my scuba certifications while I'm here. I may be gone for three months, or for more than a year. I don't know, and I don't want to know.

I've thought about this long and hard, and have been thinking about it for months now. I want a simpler life, away from LA, and away from the craziness it brings. I want to relax and de-stress. I want to be happy. And I am happy here.

Please do not try to talk me out of it, as you would just be pushing me away sooner. I've thoughts about the logistics and it will work.

The House:
I am sorry to leave you like this, but it'll be okay. We can find you a new roommate before I leave. I've already emailed Kee letting him know that I'll be gone fore three months or more doing scuba diving, and will be finding a replacement roommate.

Furniture:

Johnny FD

You, Kevin, and/or the new roommate can borrow all of my furniture until I return. This includes, my bed, TV, stereo equipment, microwave, table, chairs, etc.

Clothes:
I can pack up my clothes and store it at my parents house along with other small personal belongings. I can also sell off some things before I leave.

Cars:
I am planning to sell both of my cars. I you want to buy my Lexus, I will happily give you a fair price for it and work out a payment plan if needed.

Money:
I will continue to help in the three major cities. New York, San Francisco, and LA. I will work two gigs, every three months back to back and in different cities. Example: one weekend in San Francisco, then the next in New York, two months later, I will work one weekend in New York, and one in LA.

Passive Income:
I really, really, want time to concentrate on passive income. Living in Thailand without any other stress, will allow me to put two days aside to do internet work. If I can create passive income, it will help both of us.

Virtual Workload:
The goal for me moving out here is to have less stress, not more. But I understand that keeping my brand up is important as well. So I will be scheduling myself two days for internet work which includes updating my blog, and being active on forums. I will also write an article a week for your newsletter. Which by the way, I think is better to have quality over quantity.

The reason why we had such good success sending out newsletters is because we would never send them out, and when we did, they were good and people wanted to read them. Now that we are flooding email boxes three times a week with average articles, we will start losing readers.

Housing, Living, Food, Visas, Passports, etc etc.

Johnny FD

I've looked into all of it, and I'll survive. I've realized that if I try to plan everything too perfectly, it'll never get done. So as long as I know it is possible and know I can do it, I will figure it out as I go along.

Conclusion:
As you can tell, I've put a lot of time and thought into this, and my decision has been made. I know its not the best time to go out a self discovery journey, spiritual quest, or whatever you want to call this. But the time will never be perfect and at the same time, it is perfect now.

JT I love you like family. You have my loyalty and respect always. I hope you understand and I have your blessings, but even if you don't right now, I'm sorry but I have to go. I will be returning to LA on 10/28 to prepare and finish up all open business and scheduled events. My goal is to have everything completed within 60 days. I will give up my spot going to Australia to help you save money as I know you'll be worried about it for a while. But I'm confident it will all workout fine for both of us. We'll be in an even better place next year than we are now, in all aspects of our lives, career, and happiness.

Love,
Johnny

End of Letter

This photo was taken during that first trip to Thailand before I wrote the letter. I never thought I would share that letter with anyone, especially not the world, but it was such a vital part of my decision to move to Thailand that this book would not have been complete without it.

I know the majority of you aren't planning on moving here long term, you're just trying to plan a 2 to 12 week vacation where you train Muay Thai or even just explore the country. Ironically that was my exact mentality as well when I first came.

If anything if you already love Muay Thai, MMA, or Scuba Diving, then you are way ahead of me when I first came. I grew up never having a passion. I had a few hobbies here and there, but nothing I really loved. In fact, I always felt left out whenever the subject of sports was brought up or came on TV. Basketball, Football, Soccer, Boxing, Baseball, Volleyball, Racing, nothing interested me. It wasn't until I discovered Muay Thai did I start loving fighting sports and the UFC. Little did I know, my two new found passions would shape the rest of my life.

I originally came for the purpose of furthering my scuba training. Rene had mentioned after my open water class that I was a natural and should think about becoming a Dive Master. At the time I was naïve enough to think it was a privilege, almost the same as meeting Adele and having her tell you that you're a natural and you should become an Music Artist. Little did I know at that time that anyone with $1,000US and 3 months could become a DM. I'll go more into detail in chapter four regarding working as a divemaster in Thailand.

It was one of the best years of my life, I loved learning, diving, and best of all getting paid for it. In search of better diving, led me to Koh Lanta, which is a big island south west of Phuket. It was there, at Lanta Muay Thai, a small local thai gym that I first got into muay thai, and eventually had my first real fight. A fight that I both lost and gained so much from experiencing. If only I knew then the contents of this book back then, I would have won that fight, but then again, everything happens for a reason.

Here's my actual to do list that I wrote up for what I needed to complete before leaving for Thailand:

Thailand To Do List

- Talk to JT about work
- Talk to Kee about lease
- Sell Miata
- Sell Lexus
- Breakup with Laura
- Open ING Direct or HSBC Bank Account
- Sell/Give away extra stuff I don't need
- Ship clothes and extra stuff to San Francisco
- Cancel stuff
- Cancel Netflix
- Pay off Utilities – Electricity, Gas, AT&T Internet
- Buy Thailand Plane Ticket
- Pack for Thailand
- Get Tourist Visa
- Fax OCTFCU to stop taking money from my WAMU Account

I wish I could do what you're doing Johnny: my friends often say.

"Thailand looks beautiful." "Work sucks, I'm so sick of this shit." "I hate my job. I can't wait to go to Thailand." These are phrases I hear all of the time from my friends back in the U.S.

When I ask them why they don't just come now, the reasons are always either, it's not a good time. Or they need to save up some money.
But here's the thing, it's never a good time to come. It's like Heisenberg's Uncertainty Principle in a sense where it's impossible to have both an abundance of time and money at any given time. You will always be lacking one or the other. So when is the perfect time to come to Thailand? See chapter two.

I have a friend, Simon that hated his job and wanted to move and live out of the country, he was smart, he started saving and selling off his stuff. He had a plan to work for another year then live in Asia for the next two. But then one day he buys a motorcycle. I knew that was the beginning of the end to his dream. He found a hobby in the U.S. that he could now pour his energy, focus and savings into. Long story short, he never did end up moving to Asia, as most people don't. Whenever people have money burning a hole in their pocket, they find a way to spend it, it's human nature.

Another friend Chris, had a dream to move to Brazil to study Brazilian Jiu-Jitsu for six months. He hated his job, and still does, four years later. He said he had bills to pay and needed to save up money, but in the mean time, he's now four years older, has even more responsibilities and his chances of moving and fulfilling that dream become even more distant every day that passes.

Johnny FD

Chapter 2:

The Perfect time to come to Thailand.

The more time passes, the more things to come up and keep you from coming at all, making the perfect time to come, yesterday.

When I went back to the states to plan my trip I gave myself six months to save money, sell off my things and make the move. But with everyday that passed, every person I spoke to, I had ten new reasons not to go. It really angered me as I knew in the bottom of my heart that this was a wise move and it would make me happy, but every single person I told about my trip would shoot me down and give me reasons why I shouldn't go. This list included people that really had no say in my life, even they gave me a hard time. One of my best friends for years pulled me aside and suggested I go on antidepressants or at least go see a shrink. Luckily I was strong enough to ignore his advice. Other friends, would try to scare me by talking about the dangers, or bring up things that really didn't matter right now but would still worry me.

It seemed like everyone was against me, every single person had ten reasons why I shouldn't go, and this was only for a three month trip at the time! It wasn't even my family that was giving me a hard time, I hadn't even told them yet, it was random acquaintances that I told just to be polite. What makes me sad is I'm sure, all of them were secretly hoping for me to fail, for me to either heed their advice and stay, or better yet go to Thailand and come back with my tail between my legs, saying it didn't work out or wasn't what I expected. Maybe then, they would have felt better about their own lives. Thinking back, those same people that told me not to come four years ago, are their lives better off now than before?

Of my best friends from college had many chances to come and I know for a fact that he would have absolutely loved it here. He would have been happy as hell, as he loves Muay Thai even more than I do. But he had excuses, his parents need him to help out at their business once in a while, he has responsibilities. The funny thing is, he thinks he's somehow unique in his situation. But he's not, he just never broke the chains of his overbearing parents. Looking at what he's actually accomplished in the past four years, he had a business that did okay and he gained some valuable experience from that. He got to finally move to San Francisco where he's always wanted to live and got to live in the heart of Los Angeles as well. He had a girlfriend for a while, and even though it didn't work out, it was a good experience for him. Now he's working on another business which hopefully will be successful. He finally bought his dream car that he wanted since college, but I can tell it doesn't truly makes him happy as it's just a material thing. But when it comes down to it, he's now four years older, in worse shape, single, and life is literally passing him by.

If he had taken the savings he had when started or when he sold his share in his first business and came to Thailand, he would today be in the best shape of his life, have a girlfriend, and do what he loves doing, I know it. I have a feeling that he would have started a different business while he was out here, maybe something related to Muay Thai which he loves. I also would have had one of my best friends here with me and together we would have been unstoppable. My entire life I've always heard people older than me tell me how important time and my youth is, and I've always ignored them, just like I'm sure 22 year old's do now when I tell them the same thing. But now that I'm 31, I absolutely know what they are talking about. Our time and our youth is truly precious and it flies by faster and faster every year. What ever your age is right now, make the most of it and don't waste another year hoping, dreaming or putting off what you really want to do.

I don't know what your personal situation is, but I want you to think back on the last four years of your life and honestly ask yourself if you truly spent it wisely

Compared to yourself 4 years ago:

- Are you in better shape?
- Are you married to someone you passionately love?
- Did you learn another language?
- Did you live in another culture?
- Do you have less debt and bills or do you have more?
- Do you have more money in your savings account?
- Did you build a company or a career that is your passion?
- Did you master any skills or hobbies?

For some of you, your life is better off because you stayed at home and worked towards what you are doing now. My sister for an example had a great, productive last four years with her house, business, children and husband. However, I'm willing to bet that the majority of us, didn't really do all that much in the past four years. Sure we traveled a bit, but do 1 week vacations really count a seeing a country? We may have had a few relationships but if they didn't end up being the love of your life, wouldn't it to have been more exciting as having a fling with someone totally not from your culture? The one thing I think about most every time I see someone in their youth is how good I would be at Muay Thai today if I had started at their age. Nothing, truly nothing is a substitution for time.

In the past four years since I first decided to come, I am in far better shape and overall more healthy, plus I can kick my 27 year old's ass. I didn't get married or meet the love of my life but I did learn what love feels like so I know what to look for now. I also had some really good long term relationships and also a bunch of really exciting flings which I'll talk about in Chapter 4. As far as languages go, my Mandarin, Chinese went from being really basic to being really fluent from teaching scuba diving in Mandarin for a year. I also learned some basic Thai during that time and a surprising decent about of Spanish.

I ended up living in most of Thailand, in Malaysia, in the Caribbeans, spending a month in Guatemala and finally got to live my dream of living on a small remote tropical island. As far as money, it's a bit ironic but I'm technically richer now that I was four years ago as I paid off my student loans, car payments and have zero debt anywhere. Up until recently I always had at least $5,000US in my savings account, which I thought was perfectly normal until I found out, even my "richest" friends back home really live paycheck to paycheck. As far as career goes, I've built something I truly love, a website that people actually read and look forward to visiting, and I finally wrote my first book. In that time I've mastered scuba diving, and became quite decent at Muay Thai. All in all, these past four years I've lived, learned and done more than I ever would have if I had stayed home. All while not racking up any debt, getting in better shape and making really good friends all around the world.

Even though most of you will plan to come for less than three months, I'm going to explain things with the idea that there's a possibility that you might come for longer. Mainly because for most people, leaving their job and home for three months seems like such a big deal, it might as well be three years. The second reason why I'm going to explain a lot of things with the mentality of longer trips is because many of you will end up either extending your trip while you're here, or planning another trip the minute you get home.

There are however, better seasons to come to Thailand than others. I was previously totally unaware and ended up moving to Koh Tao in the only month that the island is uninhabitable. I was in Phuket in October, the weather was beautiful, dry and sunny. It was like a perfect summer. I went home to sell all of my stuff and came back three weeks later, this time to Koh Tao. I had no idea that November is monsoon season there, which meant all the restaurants were shut and I had no where to eat. Within days the island's roads started flooding up to knee level and it was impossible to even walk some places. The funny thing is, I didn't regret it for a second. Just the fact that I had left my stressful life back in America and was living freely in Thailand, I loved it.

I ended up meeting two girls from New Zealand that were both stuck on the island at the same time as me. Boramy and Irene, and ended up taking an overnight train up to Chiang Mai together. It was fun, we each had our own sleeping berths and stayed up late playing games and telling riddles. Even though it was four years ago, I still remember it vividly as it was my first trip as a free man within Thailand. The weather in the north was perfect, it didn't rain at all and life as we know it was fantastic. It was also the start of the political crisis in Thailand, the whole red shirt verses yellow shit debate. They closed down all of the international airports and Boramy and hundreds of others were stuck in Thailand and couldn't return home. I thought, great, you now have an excuse why you can stay in Thailand another week or two. Just tell your boss that you're safe but can't get a plane home, he'll hear about it all over the news anyways.

It wasn't just her. Everyone I met was glued to the news and constantly read updated articles online about the situation. We were in zero danger, had perfect weather and was in a beautiful part of Thailand. I'm willing to bet that within a week of them getting home and getting back to work, they all regretted not staying longer. They all wished they were back in Thailand.

Even during the Thailand floods everyone heard about, life went on pretty much as normal for most of the country. It's like if there is a riot or an earthquake in Los Angeles, it really doesn't affect people in Texas or New York. The great thing about Thailand is because it's such a big country with two very different weather seasons, anytime of the year there is summer, somewhere.

In Chiang Mai and Bangkok, the weather doesn't change enough to base your travel plans around it. The weather is always going to be hot, 33c is 91 degrees Fahrenheit. So basically the highs will range from 90 to 96 degrees. It'll always be hot. And at night it'll never drop below 60 degrees Fahrenheit. As for rain fall, some months it'll rain a lot more than others, but you have to realize that rain in Thailand is much different from rain back home

Monthly averages Chiang Mai			°C
January	Avg low: 15°	Avg hi: 30°	Avg precip: 0.33 cm
February	Avg low: 16°	Avg hi: 33°	Avg precip: 0.95 cm
March	Avg low: 20°	Avg hi: 35°	Avg precip: 1.77 cm
April	Avg low: 23°	Avg hi: 36°	Avg precip: 3.85 cm
May	Avg low: 24°	Avg hi: 34°	Avg precip: 12.58 cm
June	Avg low: 24°	Avg hi: 32°	Avg precip: 8.87 cm
July	Avg low: 24°	Avg hi: 32°	Avg precip: 10.49 cm
August	Avg low: 24°	Avg hi: 32°	Avg precip: 16.07 cm
September	Avg low: 23°	Avg hi: 32°	Avg precip: 15.67 cm
October	Avg low: 22°	Avg hi: 31°	Avg precip: 8.51 cm
November	Avg low: 19°	Avg hi: 30°	Avg precip: 3.9 cm
December	Avg low: 16°	Avg hi: 28°	Avg precip: 1.18 cm

In Phuket, the temperatures are also similar, they don't range very much, it's pretty much hot all year and some months like September it rains a lot more often.

Back home when it rains, it sucks. It's cold, dark, depressing and uncomfortable. In Thailand it'll most likely still be hot and sunny when it rains and it's actually refreshing most of the time. It's actually really nice to train Muay Thai while it's raining outside. Since the gyms are indoor/outdoor, it'll be a lot cooler. You'll hear the rain fall on the metal roofs and look out to see all the greenery get watered.

Sometimes I've even ran out after practice into the rain to do pushups. It felt amazing, and it was something I never would have done back home.

AVERAGE PHUKET WEATHER	JAN	FEB	MAR	APR	MAY	JUN	JUL	AG	SE
Daily max temp. in Deg. C	32	33	34	33	32	31	31	31	30
Nightly min temp. in Deg. C	21	23	24	26	25	24	24	24	23

When not to come to Thailand:

The only two places in Thailand that absolutely shut down certain months of the year are Koh Tao on the east coast and Koh Lanta on the west. The reason for it isn't even just the weather, as you could still train muay thai there without much problem. It's because the waves are too high to get supplies on and off the island easily and mainly because scuba diving, snorkeling, and other boat tours would be impossible during those times. So for Koh Tao, November is the month to avoid. For Koh Lanta, the island shuts down their scuba diving operations from May – October. I would also try to avoid Koh Samui and Koh Phangan (the full moon party island) in November as it's right next to Koh Tao and has the same monsoon.

You could potentially still visit these islands during those months but risk having most restaurants and shops closed and not much else to do. As for Phuket, Chiang Mai, Pattaya, Bangkok, and the rest of Thailand, aside from being a bit hot or a bit rainy some months more than others, anytime of the year is fine to go, especially if you're just there to do Muay Thai.

In Chiang Mai there is a rice field burning season that starts around February 15th – April 1st where the air quality can get really bad some days. The biggest issue isn't just the smoke that covers the air, it's that it traps all of the car exhaust smoke. Unfortunately Thailand doesn't enforce smog laws a lot of cars, especially tuk-tuks and trucks spew tons of toxic exhaust smoke which gets trapped under the blanket of smoke from the burning. It makes it difficult to run outdoors, gives people respiratory problems and makes it hot and stuffy. Everything in Chiang Mai is still open during this season, including all of the gyms, but if you have the choice I would avoid it even though you can technically train through it. However, I would definitely try to come back to Chiang Mai for Songkran, which is around April 16th which is the most amazing festival in the world. It is literally a nation wide water fight, and it's far more fun in Chiang Mai than anywhere else. You can read more about the burning season by doing a search on my blog for it.

Responsibilities, bills, and other reasons why you're not already here.

The best thing I did in preparation to come to Thailand, even just for the first three week trip was the "Elimination" chapter in the 4-hour workweek.
My typical day used to consist of waking up in a rush to hurry to work. Picking up some fast food or chinese takeout on the way to the office, showing my face and then checking my email. If nothing was too urgent, I'd reward myself by browsing the internet, checking facebook, personal email, and wasting a few hours on various forums having arguments with 12 year olds on who would win in a fight Bruce Lee or Georges St. Pierre. Then it was time to browse the deal of the day websites for things to order online.

After lunch, I would try to get some actual work done, but most of it consisted of making calls, leaving voice mails, checking voice mails, and updating excel spreadsheets. By the time I got home at night I would be too tired to go to the gym. The highlight of my day was coming home to another UPS package on my door step. It was like Christmas everyday, especially since I'd often forget what I had actually ordered the week before. The weekends were reserved for chores, relaxing watching DVDs and going out to eat with friends and drinking, a lot of drinking. Doing laundry, shopping, cleaning the apartment, paying bills, hitting the bars, you know the usual.

Then I decided to stop doing all of it. It's funny how much you can eliminate from your life once you decide what's really important. The first thing I did was cancel my netflix subscription and everything else I didn't really need. Next I truly automated my bill paying. My goal was to be able to leave for six weeks without having to worry about anything. I wanted to cut down on the amount of emails and voice mails I received. I decided zero was a good number so I promptly changed my voice mail greeting to:

"Hi, you've reached Johnny. Please do not leave a voice mail as I will only be checking it once a week from now on. Instead, please send me an email to johnny_something_at_gmail.com. Or better yet, send me a text message for an immediate response."

I also put my email to vacation mode with an auto reply and created a new email address for immediate response. The vacation auto responder said:

"Message not received: Please read for Johnny's new email address

Hi, you've reached Johnny's email. Sorry I did not receive it. If you have an order to place please contact: sales_at_yadayada.com

If you have any questions or need advice please create a post at the forums at: yada yada / forums at advice_dot com.

If you still need to reach me, please send an email to my new email address Johnny_Overseas_at_mail_dot com and I will reply every Monday and Thursday. If this is an urgent matter, please call me on my cellular phone at 415-111-1111

Warm Regards,

Johnny

----End of Autoresponder---

Overnight, I went from 40 emails a day to 2. The number of voice mails went down to exactly 0, with the exception of my mom who would leave one anyways regardless of what my greeting said. And the calls and text message I got were actually ones I wanted to get instead of mindless dribble. Instantly, I had freed up hours of my day.

Next, I started selling all the crap that was cluttering my apartment, things I didn't really need. More importantly I stopped buying all the things I didn't need in the first place. Turns out, it's a hundred times easier to save $20 by not buying something in the first place than to try to sell something for $10 on craigslist. The book Rich Dad, Poor Dad really changed my mentality of how to think about money.

With my newly found free time, and minimalistic lifestyle, I started actually working when I was at work. I stopped online shopping, visiting forums, and surfing the web. I actually started making pretty good money, best of all, I wasn't spending nearly as much in the first place. My bank account started looking good for my first trip to Thailand, I had saved up around $3,000US in the matter of months and automated my life to a point where I knew I didn't have to check email, pay bills or even answer calls unless I wanted to.

It wasn't until I went to Thailand did I truly understand what living minimalistic meant. Instead of wearing nice clothes, expensive shoes and driving a high end car, I was wearing flip flops, shorts, and a $3 t-shirt I bought from the night market. I didn't need a car as taxis were so cheap and abundant everywhere I couldn't walk to. I found out that Rene lived in a hotel room and paid monthly for it, contract free.

I asked myself, how cool would that be! Not having to worry about furniture, bills, or even cleaning up after myself. I didn't need a kitchen as food in Thailand is so cheap and it's common to just walk down the street and have breakfast, lunch or dinner. I decided that this easy going, stress free life was definitely for me and during those three weeks back in the U.S. I really pushed the "Elimination" chapter to it's fullest. I sold, donated and gave away everything.

A list of things you MUST do before you come.
First and foremost, eliminate what bills you can, then automate the remainders. One of the biggest wastes of money while you're away is paying rent in an unused apartment. See if you can take this opportunity to end your lease and move yourself into storage until you get back. The best storage is free storage so hopefully you're on good terms with your parents. For me, I took the plunge and got rid of everything expect for three boxes of keepsakes and winter clothes. One box was my DVD collection, which in hindsight was a complete waste of a box as everything is downloadable now.

Put your stuff in Storage:
If you must store your things find the cheapest storage possible, I used a service where they deliver a huge metal shipping container pod to my front door, I filled it up and they picked it up a day later to stack on top of other units. The downside to these pods are since they are stacked on top of each other, you don't

have easy access to them like other storage units. But the great thing about them is you can still call ahead to get things out of it, or better yet, just have them deliver it to your new apartment when you get back, saving you moving trucks. I packed up my container in Orange County, and had them deliver it up to Los Angeles, about an hour away for no additional charge.

Okay so I know some of you are only going to Thailand for 2 weeks and don't want to pack up your whole life for it. In that case, still try to eliminate and automate your life as much as possible before you come. There is a 50% chance that once you're in Thailand, training Muay Thai, MMA, traveling or scuba diving, doing what you love, you'll want to either extend your trip or stay indefinitely. Trust me, I've met hundreds of guys at the camps here and I would say that at least 20% just say fuck it and stay longer than they planned regardless of any preparation on their part. So even if you don't plan on staying longer than planned, it's a good idea to have it be an option just in case.

Sublet your apartment:
If you're going to be gone for 1 month or longer, sublet your apartment. It's a huge waste of money to pay rent while you're away. If you're worried about your things, it's still cheaper to spend $100 and put all your things in storage for a month than it would be to pay a full months rent to the keep peace of mind that no one's touching your stuff.

If you own your house and are paying a mortgage, hire an agent or manager to look after your rental property while you're away. Three months of rent is huge and even if you're giving 10% to your manager you're still way ahead. Don't be lazy and leave your house empty while you're away, put your stuff in storage and rent it out while you're gone. The act of putting your stuff in storage is a fantastic way to gauge what you really need and to eliminate the things you don't.

Visas and Passport:
If you're reading this and you don't have a valid passport, stop and do it now. If you wait until the last minute, you'll have to pay all sorts of crazy expedite fees and overnight shipping. You'll need a passport that's valid for at least 6 months from your last entry. To play it safe make sure your passport is valid for at least another year and if you have the option when renewing it, get one with extra pages as visa runs will quickly fill it up with stamps.
Even if you think you're only going to be in Thailand for less than a month don't settle for the free 30 day on arrival visa. Spend the $30 and get a 2 month tourist visa instead. This gives you 60 days with the option to extend it for another 30 without leaving the country. I've met tons of guys who ended up staying longer and had to do annoying visa runs to Burma just to get an extra two weeks of stay. The current visa rules for most countries are you get 30 days free exemption if you arrive by airplane and if you arrive by land you get 15 days, hence the visa run to Burma.
If you see your country on this list you can technically just show up without a visa and get 30 days for free.

*48 Countries allowed to enter Thailand under the VISA EXEMPTION RULE:

Argentina
Australia
Austria
Bahrain
Belgium
Brazil
Brunei
Canada
Chile
Denmark
Finland
France
Germany
Greece
Hong Kong
Iceland
Indonesia
Ireland
Israel
Italy
Japan
Korea
Kuwait/Laos
Luxembourg
Macau
Malaysia
Monaco
Mongolia
Netherlands
New Zealand
Norway
Oman
Peru
Philippines
Portugal
Qatar
Russia
Singapore
South Africa
Spain
Sweden
Switzerland
Turkey
United Arab Emirates
United Kingdom
United States
Vietnam

If you're from any of the following countries you can get something called a Visa on arrival, which is essentially the same thing where you get 30 days, but instead of it being free it'll cost you 1,900 baht which is $63US.

*19 Countries eligible to enter Thailand under the VISA ON ARRIVAL rule:

Bhutan
China
Cyprus
Czech Republic
Estonia
Hungary
India
Kazakhstan
Latvia
Liechtenstein
Lithuania
Maldives
Mauritius
Poland
Saudi Arabia
Slovakia
Slovenia
Taiwan
Ukraine

For Tourist Visas that you apply for back home, the rules are you get 60 days with the option of going to the immigration office to extend it for another 30 days for a fee. The nice thing about it is you don't have to leave the country. They have immigration offices in Chiang Mai, Bangkok, Phuket, Koh Samui and most major cities in Thailand.

If you plan on staying for 3 months or longer, or simply want the option to stay longer, get the Multiple Entry Tourist Visa. The standard is 2 entries, which allows 60 days + 30, then another 60 days + 30 if you make a border run, giving you six months total.

Border Run vs. Visa Run:
A border run is basically leaving Thailand and coming back. The quickest easiest way is to take a minibus (minivan) to the closest bordering country, stepping off at the border and coming straight back. Because of the shape of the country, whether you're in Phuket, Bangkok or Chiang Mai, your closest bordering country is Myanmar, formerly known as Burma. The cost is usually around 500-800 baht ($16-$27) and takes the whole day. You get on the minibus in the morning, usually with 12 other people in cramped seats, drive to the border. Give your passport to some shady looking guy, pray that he actually comes back with it. (he usually does.) and then drive back, stopping for lunch along the way. You usually leave early in the morning and arrive back around 6pm on the same day.

A Visa run is going to another country to apply for another 60 day Tourist Visa, you can do this by going back to your home country or to Malaysia, Laos, Singapore or any other major country with a Thai Embassy.

The other option for a border run is to take a mini vacation. The great thing about Thailand is it's close to a bunch of other cheap countries with tons to see. I made it a point to visit a new country every time I needed to do a border run and it's worked out great. If you plan ahead you can buy plane tickets through the local airlines such as Air Asia for dirt cheap. I once made a border run and spent new years eve in Bali with a friend from Tiger Muay Thai for $110 US round trip! Another time I flew to Singapore to watch the Marital Combat Fights, which are now known as ONE FC. I've eve taken an overnight train to Laos and spent a week up there just for fun. When I was dating the Scandinavian girl, Lotta, we'd time our Visa runs to go together and have a romantic weekend away.

Lotta and I boarding an Air Asia flight to Kuala Lumpur

How to make your three grand last three months instead of 3 weeks.
From selling my stuff and my car, I had around $10,000 which I figured would last me around 5 months in Thailand. My goal was to fly back every three months to work for a bit and come back again. I did that the first time around, just to show everyone I was still alive. Then I started prolonging my trips home. I stayed overseas for 6 months, then on the next trip I stayed for an entire year. Ironically during that first three week trip, I blew around $3,000 stupidly. Since then I've figured out how to live and train for less than $1,000US a month and sometimes half of that.
The trick is to live like a local and think long term.

Accommodations aka your Apartment.
The apartment I'm staying in right now is 350 baht per night, around $11.66US. But instead of paying nightly, I opted to pay the monthly rate which is 4,000 baht a month ($134US), best of all it includes utilities, wifi and even once a week cleaning with new sheets, bedding and bath towels. If you do the math, paying the daily rate would have been much more than double, which means, if you're going to pay to stay somewhere for 12 nights, you might as well just pay for an entire month as it'll be the same price.

Food and Drink:
If you eat where the locals eat, expect to pay around 35-60 baht per meal which is less than $2US. If you eat where tourists eat, expect to pay between 150-200 baht per meal. And to be honest, I've grown the like the local thai food much more, there's more flavor and spices in it than the westernized versions for tourists. Breakfast is the hardest meal for most people to adjust to, as Thai's eat rice dishes similar to lunch food. Instead of wasting money getting the 150 baht tea, toast and egg American breakfast at your hotel, just learn to order eggs at your local thai restaurant, usually it's 10 baht a piece so you can have three scrambled eggs for 30 baht. $1US. A lot of people also learn to love fried rice with an egg on top for breakfast. Pork fried rice with a fried egg is my favorite and usually costs less than 60 baht, $2US.

Even though water is quite cheap it seriously adds up since you go through so much of it here, especially while training in the hot sun. A large bottle of water is anywhere between 20 baht – 30 baht depending on if you're buying it at a shop or restaurant. To refill the exact same bottle costs 1 baht. That's a 30x difference in price. Plus you're doing a favor to the environment and not wasting thousands of plastic bottles a year. Depending on where you are in Thailand you will either buy and refill 15 liter bottles or there will be machines placed around where you can refill any size container you wish. In Phuket opposite Tiger Muay Thai you buy a large water jug for 100-150 baht and refill it for 10 baht. In Chiang Mai there are machines everywhere that give you 1.5 liters of water for 1 baht.

Alcohol and Beer:
The thought of a nice cold beer on a hot day is refreshing, and beer isn't expensive here in Thailand. Usually around 50 – 100 baht depending on where you get it. $1.67-$3.30US and cocktails such as rum and coke are usually found for under 100 baht as well.

But if you plan on drinking, expect your food and drink budget to exactly double.

Personally I stopped drinking all together, first for budget reasons, and second because it hinders my gains in Muay Thai. People say that by going out and having a few drinks on Saturday night, you basically lose all of the gains you made training that entire week before. I've experimented it for myself and think they're onto something, especially when it comes to cardio. So if you're serious about getting in shape or want to stay on budget, stick to ice water. But at the end of the day, it's your vacation and it's up to you to set your own priorities. A cold beer or a glass of whiskey once in a while won't kill you.

Motorbike Rental:
You can rent a bike for around 350 baht a day or you can rent it for an entire month for 2,500 baht or less. Do the math, just like your accommodation it's much cheaper to pay per month than it is daily. Just be careful, if you crash the bike you'll end up paying up to 10,000 baht to fix it. And in some places like Koh Tao, almost every single motorbike rental shop tries to scam you by charging you for scratches, your fault or not.
If you plan on staying in Thailand for 3 months or longer, just buy a second hand bike. I did this every single time I came and ended up selling the bike for about what I paid for it or sometime even more. You can buy a cheap used second hand bike for around 10,000 baht ($333US) or a nice one for 15,000 baht ($500US) If you do the math, instead of paying 7,500 baht renting a bike for three months, and risking paying another couple thousand when you return it you might as well just buy a bike and anything you get back is profit.
If you've never owned a motorbike before, there is a 50% chance you will drop it or other wise have a minor accident. Some places are very forgiving of these things, while others, especially ones that hold your passport for deposit will charge you a lot for repairs.

My personal experience with Bikes.

1st Bike – Honda Wave – Paid 10,000 baht. Sold for 12,000 baht two months later

2nd Bike – Honda Dream – Paid 10,000 baht. Sold for 10,000 baht three months later.

3rd Bike – Honda Dream – Paid 10,000 baht. Sold for 8,000 baht six months later.

4th Bike – Yamaha Nuevro – Paid 15,000 baht. Sold for 12,000 bat four months later.

If you do the math, I basically ended up paying 3,000 baht for 15 months of bike rental which is about $6US a month, less than 10% of what I would have paid normally. Renting a bike for 15 months at 2,500baht would have costed me 37,500 baht ($1,250US).
If you're only here for 2 weeks, you might just have to pay the daily rate. But this is the reason why I always encourage people to stay for at least a month,

since it ends up costing almost exactly the same amount of money for 2 weeks in Thailand vs. staying a month.
Let's do the math just for fun, since math is fun and all.

Budget for 2 weeks in Thailand: Using Tiger Muay Thai in Phuket as an example.

Round trip Airfare from home: $1,500US (Approx)

Flight from Bangkok to the Phuket: $100US (Return)

Taxi to Gym and back to Airport: $40US

2 weeks unlimited training: 6,000 baht - $200US

2 weeks hotel room: 12,000 baht $400US (Floraville or other hotel near the gym)

Total: **$2,240 US**

A lot of people don't factor in the airfare in the budget, but that's the biggest part of it! Factor that shit in.

Budget for One Month in Thailand: Using Tiger Muay Thai as an example.

Round trip Airfare from home: $1,500US (Approx)

Flight from Bangkok to the Phuket: $100US (Approx – Return)

Taxi to Gym and back to Airport: $40US

1 month unlimited training: 10,000 baht - $333 US

1 Month hotel room: 15,000 baht $500US (Floraville or other hotel near the gym)

Total: **$2,473 US**

If you compare the two breakdowns, staying in the exact same hotel, everything else being equal, it's only going to cost you $233US more to stay for twice as long. That's crazy! If you start factoring in things like renting a motorbike and food it'll actually be even cheaper.

The reason why I left food out of the budget is because you have to spend money on food when you're back home anyways, and it's actually far cheaper to eat out 4 times a day in Thailand than it would be to eat at home back in the U.S. Unless of course you live with your parents still, but then again that's even more reason to get out of the house and come travel and train.

Even if you're not coming to Thailand to do Muay Thai or MMA and are just here to travel, it's still a far better deal for you to get the most out of that crazy expensive airfare, come and stay for a while. Life really shouldn't be rushed.

What to Pack: Things to bring with you to Thailand

The first time I went to Thailand I was totally unprepared, or maybe I was a bit over prepared. I brought way too much stuff that I ended up not really needing, and forgot some necessities instead. Luckily, I had my cousin coming to visit me and I had a list of things for him to bring me from the U.S. as well as take back with him.

First lets start with the luggage itself. The first trip out here, I brought the typical large rolling luggage that worked fine for me during trips to New York, Miami and even Australia. However, for Thailand it pretty much sucked. Because normal gas is expensive, most Taxi cabs in Thailand, have a CNG (Compressed Natural Gas) conversion which takes up half of the trunk. Imagine trying to fit a large rectangular luggage into the trunk of that thing.

Luggage:

Then imagine trying to walk through the messed up sidewalks and busy streets of Thailand rolling one of those things around. If you haven't been to Asia yet, try rolling a large suit case around Chinatown, it's a similar experience. The worst was trying to roll it down the broken wooden pier to take a ferry to the islands. So what do I recommend instead? Take a 75 to 95 liter hiking style backpack with you instead. The one I have is an 85 + 10 liter pack which would be way too heavy to walk around with if you were actually going camping but it's perfect for filling up and walking short distances with around Thailand while traveling.

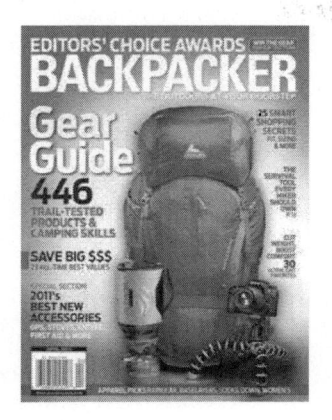

Day Pack:
I also carry a small day pack on the plane with me with my laptop, kindle, mp3 player and light weight hooded jumper for when it gets cold on planes, trains, boats and buses. In my day pack I also carry a pair of shorts, extra t-shirt, my toothbrush, and other things I would need my first night. The reason is often you'll have a lay over on your way to your final destination. It saves you from having to unpack your main luggage and is handy just in case your luggage gets lost.
I also packed a nylon drawstring bag, they weigh nothing and fold into any pocket, yet they come in really handy when going to the store or for a hike.

Clothing:
Don't bring too much clothes, it'll weigh you down and you'll end up wanting room to buy souvenirs while you're here. Technically, you can show up with nothing but the clothes on your back and buy everything here for half the price as you would back home.
I however, started really appreciating the quality of clothes we have in the U.S. after living in Asia for the last few years. Now I travel with everything I'm going to wear, with the exception of leaving room for a few t-shirts that I know I'll want to pick up.

Head – I brought with me 2 dri-fit featherlite Nike running hats. It's really sunny in Thailand and I wear them while running, hiking and even just walking around most of the day. I like these in particular because they're light weight, dry fast and are well made.

Torso – I brought two Northface vaporwick synthetic t-shirts with me. They keep me cool, are light weight and dry quickly. I wish I would have brought a third one they're so good. If you're on an island, you'll end up wearing tank tops most of the time, you can either bring a few or buy them when you're here. Combined with the cotton hooded jumper in my day pack, you should never get cold, even up in the northern mountain areas of Chiang Mai.

Underwear:
17 countries. 6 weeks. One pair of award-winning underwear. (Ok, maybe two.) That's the slogan for Ex-Officio Give-N-Go Boxers. These are amazing. Instead of lugging around 7 pairs of boxers that are a pain in the ass to wash and dry, I've been traveling the last year with just two. I wear one on the plane and have one in my bag, that's it. I actually brought a third pair with me on this trip just in case, but as you can see it still has it's tag on it. They are truly that good. They keep you cool, wick away moisture, have a Microbe Shield to eliminate odor-causing bacteria, are super comfortable and extremely quick-drying. I normally just hang them up in the sun, switching off between the two pairs, then wash them in the sink with my Muay Thai shorts after training.

Rain/Wind - I also brought a Brooks light weight running jacket with me, it's both wind and rain resistant which is perfect for wearing while riding your motorbike especially at night. Even though Thailand is quite hot usually, when you're riding on a motorbike, it gets chilly quick.

Legs – I wear a pair of long pants with me on the plane ride over. I used to wear long hiking pants that can be turned into shorts. But then I never really used them the rest of the trip. This trip, I wore a comfortable pair of jeans instead. Even if think you're going to eat, sleep, and train like a fighter. You'll end up going out at least one or two weekends a month and you'll wish you had a pair of jeans.
I also bring two pairs of shorts, as these are what you'll be wearing day to day. Get the ones that have at least one zippered pocket (sometimes it's hidden) that way you don't get pick pocketed while traveling.

Shoes – Depending where you are in Thailand, you might end up wearing flip flop sandals 99% of the time. You can buy knock off Havaianas here for around 150-200 baht ($6.60US) but they wear out after about a month of daily use. I'd much rather just buy a real pair of sandals before you come. I personally bought a pair of basic Lacoste thongs for $10 online before I came and they haven't worn down at all.

You'll also want a pair of running shoes, as you'll be doing a lot of running for Muay Thai. To save room and weight bring ankle socks instead of full length ones, I brought 6 pairs which was more than enough for me. You could get away with less if you wash them yourself.

If you're into barefoot style running and plan on bringing your Vibram Five Fingers, like I did, bring enough toe socks if you use them because they're not available in Thailand. You might also want to bring a pair of easy to put on normal shoes just to walk around in. The basic rule of thumb is if you live on an island, such as Phuket or anything that begins with Koh (which means island in Thai) you can most likely get away with just flip flops and running shoes. If you're going to be living in Chiang Mai or Bangkok, you'll also want a normal pair of shoes for everyday wear.

*Side note: Benefits of barefoot style running include minimizing knee, and back injuries, and building up strength around your ankles and foot which is great for Muay Thai and MMA. Caution, don't try to run barefoot right away, for me it took me almost three months of walking a few times a week in them to get used to it. The benefit now is the last three times I would have sprained my ankle falling on and twisting my ankle, I was completely fine, as it is stronger now.

Supplements:
Even though there are now a few GNCs around Thailand, prices are double what you would pay back home and some things are hard to come by. It's tempting to over load your bag with everything from creatine, NO-explode, to ZMA, but what I would suggest is just bring what you are currently using and what you really need. Here is a list of what I personally brought and what I recommend from highest priority to lowest.

Fish Oil Capsules - I buy the 500 count at Costco for around $10US which is 1/10 of the price you would pay for them in Thailand. I take one after each meal to counter balance all the omega 6 that I eat from the vegetable oil they use in Thai cooking. It also helps with fat loss and a host of other health benefits including joint health which is very important if you do MMA or Muay Thai.

Protein Powder – I brought a 5lb (2.25kg) tub of ON Gold Standard Whey – Chocolate with me which is 74 servings. I choose the brand Optimum Nutrition because I read a study where they compared 10 popular protein powders and found out that most of them don't have nearly as much protein as advertised, ON is true to their strength.

Vitamin C – I bought 500 chewable pills from Costco for around $10US and eat one or two for dessert after meals, instead of having something sweet like I normally crave. Plus Vit C has tons of health benefits and I hate a large dose if I feel like I'm getting sick, which often happens after being on an airplane for 20 hours.

Ibuprofen – Often known as vitamin I, Ibuprofen is an anti-inflammatory that you'll be happy you have on hand each time you hurt yourself in practice. It helps with back pain, pulled muscles, headaches and just about everything. Try not to take them unless you absolutely have to, as studies have shown you don't gain as much muscle after a workout if you take ibuprofen. I bought a 750 pill bottle at Costco for $10US which is the equivalent price of getting 50 pills at the pharmacy here in Thailand.

Caffeine Tablets – I brought a bottle from home for three reasons. First is taking it first thing in the morning the week you arrive helps you counter jet-lag. I also take one before training instead of a preworkout product. Caffeine is thought to delay the onset of muscle fatigue by helping your body use its own fat reserves as energy instead. I might also take a caffeine pill instead of drinking a red bull, if I'm going to go out at night and don't want to drink. You'll have to bring it from home as it is illegal to buy in Thailand, which ironically is also the home of Red Bull.

Pink Himalayan Salt – This is a kind of random thing but really helps. When you train a lot, you often get adrenal fatigue, and the easiest way to combat it is to simply have a teaspoon of salt in the morning with some water. It makes me have more energy throughout the day, instantly wakes me up and keeps me hydrated. The reason why I use pink himalyayan salt instead of normal white salt is first, normal salt tastes like crap, trying to drink it in the morning makes me want to throw up. The pink stuff is a finishing salt and actually tastes good, plus it contains 84 minerals that normal refined white salt doesn't have. I bought mine at Trader joes, as the only place in Thailand that sells it is the upscale Rimping supermarket which isn't in most places.

Optional Snacks:
As much as you plan on eating clean while you're training in Thailand, you won't. One of the fighters currently training at my gym, Mirkko runs 10+km a day and trains morning and afternoon. He then goes to the shop to buy ice cream, cookies and chocolate. When you train at this high of a level your body just craves calories and often meals are not enough. So might as well bring some healthy snacks with you from home, as they are hard to find here in Thailand and often a lot more expensive.
I personally brought 3lbs of Raw Almonds, and 15 bars of dark chocolate. I figure I'm going to eat snacks anyways, I might as well have it be somewhat healthy. I also found drinking protein shakes, especially if you mix it with a bit of coconut milk (cheaply available in Thailand and super good for you) satisfies most of my cravings. On my next trip I plan on bringing some beef jerky as well.

Sundries and Toiletries -
You can buy everything in Thailand, often for less money than you would back home with the exception of the following items:

Neosporin – This handy antibiotic ointment has a patent that makes cuts heal. There are tons of antibiotic creams in Thailand but none of them actually close up your wounds. I brought three tubes with me as you get cuts, scrapes, and infections all of the time in Thailand, especially while training.

Sunblock – Thais don't use sunblock, which is ironic because they love to be light skinned. Which means, sunblock is a luxury item and costs 3x as much as it does back home. Often there will be whitening bleach in the sunblock here as well, which can't be good for your skin.

Tampons and Condoms – Two things that aren't readily available or cheap in Thailand, bring your own.

Natural Products – I personally brought all of my own toothpaste, shampoo, deodorant and soap with me as I like to use natural products without a bunch of chemicals in it. I remember when I was 13 years old and buying my first stick of deodorant, I asked what the difference between anti-perspirant and deodorant was. When I found out anti-perspirant stops you from sweating, I thought to

myself, "that can't be good for you." 15 years later, studies come out showing that the aluminum in it causes cancer.
The choice is yours, it's your body, but personally I'd rather use products that don't have a bunch of chemicals, artificial scents, colors and other crap I can't pronounce in it. I personally use:

Tom's Natural's – For deodorant and toothpaste (bought anywhere)

Dr. Bronner's 18 in 1 Peppermint Soap – For shampoo, face soap, body wash, fruit wash and shave cream. (bought at trader joes)

Muay Thai and MMA Gear -
You can either bring your gear from home or buy a new set here in Thailand. Here you'll get authentic, high quality, hand made Thai equipment for a good price. The cheapest place to buy gear in Thailand is in Bangkok at Action Zone or at the Boon store.
In Phuket go to the Phuket Fight Store which is half way between Tiger Muay Thai and Phuket Top Team in Phuket.
In Chiang Mai, there is a tiny Twins Shop in the Night market, a stall that makes custom Muay Thai shorts for 750 baht ($25US) on the same side of the street to the right if you're coming out of the Twins shop, and a small shop next to the Loi Kroh market that has a bit more selection. Santai Muay Thai also has a gear shop at their gym where they sell Fairtex stuff.
Bangkok has the cheapest prices by far, and Phuket second. Even though everything else in Chiang Mai is dirt cheap, the Muay Thai gear isn't as there isn't much competition or volume there. Only the custom fight shorts are cheap in Chiang Mai.

Mouth Guard – This is the most important piece of gear for sparring and fighting. At the very least get a cheap boil in hot water one. Personally I invested around $90US in a custom molded, dental quality one. If you are going to fight seriously, get one. Your teeth are important and if it wasn't for my high end mouth piece, I'm almost positive I would have lost some teeth in my last fight where I got elbowed in the mouth a few times.
Other benefits of a custom mouth guard include being able to talk more clearly while it's in verses cheap ones. This comes in handy during sparring in between rounds. One big benefit is that it makes it a lot easier to breathe as it doesn't fall out when you open your mouth. You can take those big breaths even with it in. This really helped me when I got a bloody nose once in the middle of a round and had to breathe with my mouth instead of through my nose.

Gloves – Get two pairs if you can. A pair of 16oz gloves for sparring and a pair of 12oz gloves for bag and pad work. If you're a girl or guy under 60kg 14oz gloves are fine for sparring but for most guys it's unfair to your partner if he's using 16oz gloves and you're in 14s. It's easier to accidentally injure your sparring partner in smaller gloves, especially if you aren't in control of your emotions, and you'll punch faster and harder than the guy in 16s. The reason to get lighter gloves for pads and bags is because you end up having bad form when your gloves are too heavy, especially when you get tired.

My favorite brand, by far is Fairtex. I spent a week using different brands of gloves including Twins, Boons, and Top King and ended up liking the Fairtex ones the best. I trained in a high end pair of Everlasts the first six months and they fell apart. Whatever you end up getting, make sure it's leather and not synthetic.

Shin Guards – Fit is extremely important so make sure you try them on. You want them tight as one of the biggest annoyances is having to adjust it while you're sparring, both for you and your partner.

These are used solely for sparring. You'll like like an idiot using them to kick pads or the bag. If you are a beginner and you have sensitive shins just kick lightly for the first month and it'll naturally toughen up. Muay Thai ligament oil and ice helps as well.

Hand Wraps – My favorite are a pair of 180" Mexican hand wraps from Ringside that my friend Jason gave me that finally wore out after two years. Now I'm using a pair of Revgear elastic hand wraps which I heard may be from the same manufacture. The benefit of elastic is without it, often one hand will often feel tighter than the other, with elastic you don't get that problem. I also have a pair of throwdown wraps that are too narrow and not very well made, I do not recommend those. Also make sure you hang your wraps every day after training to dry, and make sure you wash them at least once a week.

Muay Thai Shorts – While it's possible just to wear normal workout shorts during practice, it's part of the uniform and it's just something you should do out of respect and also to not look like it's your first day of class. I recommend getting a pair made out of traditional satin which is what most brands in Thailand use. I still wear my first pair of Muay Thai satin shorts made by Intern on a daily basis now for three years and they still look great. A pair of Muay Thai shorts I bought in America was made out of Nylon and are terrible. First most Nylon shorts are see through, (I don't wear underwear under my shorts) and second they get really hot and clingy when you sweat. Go with Satin to be safe.

Mesh Duffle Bag – It's a good idea to bring a light weight, breathable mesh duffle bag to put all your gym equipment in. Even if you life at or near the gym, it's much easier to keep all your belongings in one place to to try to carry gloves, shin pads, bottles of water and everything else you'll need.

Electronics – First off, realize the voltage in Thailand in 220volts so before you bring any electronics to Thailand, look at the back, usually on the power supply to see if it is compatible. In the U.S. our voltage is 110v but many electronics are 110-240v switching. Don't worry about the actual plugs itself as all surge protectors in Thailand come built in with multiple inputs (genius really). By the way, make sure you use a surge protector for everything. It's ironic that we use them in the U.S. for everything and hardly ever get actual surges or brown outs, maybe once every 10 years. But it happens weekly in Thailand so use one. You can buy them anywhere they sell electronics in Thailand for less than 100 baht ($3US) such as Big C or Tesco Lotus.

Electronic Beard Trimmer – If you use a beard trimmer at home like I do, bring a battery powered one with you. Most bathrooms in Thailand don't have power outlets, so you'll want one that is cordless. Mine uses AA batteries which is easy to find here.

Laptop – Perfect for watching movies, gaming, going online and skyping when you're not training. If you're staying in Thailand for more than 1 month, I would recommend bringing a laptop. If you're here for 3 months or more, it's a requirement. Oh yeah and bring a mouse too, I recommend the Logitech M125 Corded Mouse as it doesn't need to be recharged or use batteries.

Kindle – I used to prefer paper back books, until I started using a kindle. It weighs less than a single book, and can hold hundreds. The problem with bookstores in Thailand is you most likely won't find what you want. Chiang Mai is the only city in Thailand with a decent used book store, and if you're looking for new books, you'll have a hard time. What I like about my kindle is I can download books on the day it comes out for half the price of buying a hard copy. Plus the battery lasts up to 4 weeks on a single charge, that's crazy!

Iphone/iPad/iPod Touch/Tablet: If you already have one, load it up with games, podcasts and things you can do offline. It's a great way to pass the time on airplane journeys and long bus rides. I don't use my iPhone to make calls in Thailand, I bought a cheap 750 baht ($25US) Nokia for that, since I often bring it to the beach and other places it can break. If you don't have one yet, I would recommend either an iPod Touch or a Google Nexus 7 Tablet. It's definitely optional but it's nice for plane rides and visa runs.

Mp3 Player – Primary used for running, you may also be asked to plug yours into the gym's stereo for music during training. I personally love my iPod shuffle. It's small, lightweight, has a built in clip, and costs only $50US.

Running Headphones – I used to use standard ear buds but they would always fall out while running, especially when I started sweating. Then I discovered Yurbuds Inspire Duro, they are seriously the best ear buds I've ever used in my life. Great sound quality and the unique twist lock head, where you physically twist them into your ear, makes it so they never fall out, even when I sweat.

External Speaker – I brought along an x-mini speaker. It's tiny, rechargeable, and is perfect for listening to music or watching movies in my room. I used to carry around bigger laptop speakers, but this little thing works better and is literally the size of a golf ball but has surprisingly big sound and bass. Best of all, you can daisy chain two or more of them together if you need it to be louder.

External Hard drive – This one's optional but it might be a good idea to fill up a small usb powered external hard drive with movies and TV-series. Depending on where you are in Thailand, you may or may not have fast enough internet to download large files. Places like Tiger Muay Thai block torrent downloads. Personally I ended up watching a lot more TV-series than movies out here. My favorites while being out here have been Game of Thrones, Spartacus, The Ultimate Fighter, Undercover Boss, Big Bang Theory, How I Met Your Mother, Two and a Half Men, and True Blood.

USB Memory Sticks – These are the size of a stick of gum, and come in really handy when trading pictures or movies with friends. Best of all, if your room has either a flat screen with a built in usb port, or a DVD player with a usb port, you can watch movies on your TV instead of your laptop.

Johnny FD

The crew from Phuket Top Team at Koh Phi Phi – photo taken with a Canon S95

Digital Camera – If you're going to travel all the way to Thailand, you might as well go home with some good memories. Sure you can take photos with your phone, but you'll end up taking a lot more, and better photos, especially at night with a real camera, so bring one along. I highly recommend Canon cameras. I use an S95 and love it, it's now been replaced by the S100 which is even better, and now the S110 is out.

Solar USB Charger – Not that you'll ever need to charge something with the sun, but these little things come in handy on long plane and bus rides as you can use them to charge your iPod or anything that takes usb power. You can charge them up through your laptop and use it as an external battery. This one's completely optional but they do come in handy.

Budgeting and Saving: How much you should expect to spend.

The actual living costs of a fight camp is often very different from what guys budget for. Living in Thailand can be very very cheap but there are also many ways to blow your six months savings in half that time. Here is a breakdown of actual real life costs. Here is a breakdown of what I spent while living in Phuket. The prices at Tiger Muay Thai, Phuket Top Team, Rawaii and Sinbi were all about the same plus or minus 1,000 baht ($33US)

Strict Budget - Cheapest Possible per month

Monthly Training - Muay Thai and MMA - 9,000 baht ($300US)

Accommodation: Fan Room with Shared Bathroom - 5,500 baht ($185US)

Breakfast - Eggs, Omelet or Oatmeal with Fruit - 40baht per meal x 30 = 1,200 baht ($40US)

Lunch - Thai Food - Chicken Basil with Rice, Fried Rice Chicken, Mixed Veggies with Chicken and Rice 50 baht x 30 = 1,500 baht ($50US)

Dinner – Big Chicken, Broccoli and Rice - 100 baht per meal x 30 = 3,000 baht ($100US)

Drinks - Only Water which you refill yourself from 10 liter jugs - 80 baht ($2.65US)

Entertainment - Visit temples, the big Buddha, relax on the beaches, go hiking, sneak into a resorts pool, play board games, watch TV and DVDs, internet - all free.

Total Cost for a Month of Training on a Strict Budget - 20,280 baht - $676US Dollars

*You can save $133 a month by paying for 20 classes per month instead of unlimited, which will be good for 1 class a day, 5 days week and training on your own on your off time. New total: $543 a month.

So yes, it is possible to live super cheap out here in Thailand which is what I've been doing for the past three years now on and off. After reading the book by Tim Ferris, "The 4-Hour Workweek" I decided that for the cost of one month's rent alone back in Los Angeles, I could live, train and eat out here, I made the move.

However, here are common add-ons that will eat into your budget: Some of them are necessary to live and others are out of convenience and comfort.

Pharmacy - Ibuprofen, Muscle Relaxers, Pain Killers, Anti Biotic Cream, Tiger Balm, and Re-hydration Powders (powdered Gatorade) 570 baht a month on average. $19US

Motorbike Rental - If you want to get around the island you'll most likely rent a scooter. Learn to ride a semi-automatic (manual) and save yourself tons of money, it only takes a few days to get used to. 2,000 baht a month for a manual, 3,500 for an automatic. $67-$117US a month. (Prices though Tiger Muay Thai's TKO Bike rental service higher than what you would pay through renting a Bike at Tony's restaurant, Ja-Ja's or any shop on the street.)

Tips on motorbikes: What Thai's call Manual bikes are actually semi-automatic since there is no clutch. If you are staying for three months or more, it is much cheaper to buy a 2nd hand motorbike because you can sell it when you leave for roughly the same as you paid for it. Buy a Honda Wave, Honda Dream, or a Suzuki Swift for easy repairs and resale for about 10,000baht $334US and sell it for 8,000-10,000baht when you leave.

Bicycle: Having a normal bicycle isn't very practical in Phuket unless you use it just on the street between Tony's Restaurant and Tiger Muay Thai. But on Koh Lanta and in Chiang Mai where it's relatively flat you can get away with just having a pedal bike which is what I have now in Chiang Mai. You can rent them for less than 1,000 baht per month ($33US) or you can buy one like I did at Big C Supercenter for 3,000 baht ($100US).

Massages - If you are in Thailand and you are pushing your boxing in Muay Thai and MMA, you really should treat yourself at least once a week to a Thai Massage. Prices range from 150 baht an hour if you go to local places, and up to 300 baht an hour at Phuket Spa, where you get to use their steam room, jacuzzi, and swimming pool for free. $5US - $10US per hour.

Movie Theater/Cinema - The theaters in Thailand are very nice, play new western movies in English (with thai subs) and are much cheaper than back home. On Wednesdays it's even cheaper at only 80 baht, normal price is 140 baht. $2.65-$4.65

Actual Comfortable Budget per month

Including Training, Accommodation, Food, and Extras - 24,110 baht per month including weekly massages, movies, and a motorbike. $804 US Dollars.

However, there is an evil that will kill your budget and about 50% of guys that come train Muay Thai and MMA end up falling for it. It's called Patong. If you start going there, you will not stop. Luckily most guys will only go on Saturday nights, but many end up going a few times a week. Here's what to add to your budget if you do.

Taxi - 100 baht there, and 500 baht return, as going there you'll be in a big group but coming back you'll usually be solo or with one other person. $20US

Motorbike Accident - If you think you'll save money driving there, you have a big chance of getting into an accident, even if you only have one or two drinks. 20,000 baht or more. $666US.
Alcohol - Drinks are a bit cheaper in Thailand than back home. But if you compare it to food it's actually really expensive and it's terrible for your training. 60baht per drink $2US. Which doubles your food budget.

Strippers, Bar Girls, Whores - If you're a single guy, drinking in Patong, after spending all week with a bunch of dudes in a house training, you spending 2,000 baht won't seem like such a bad idea. $67US.

Actual Monthly Cost if you go to Patong once a week - 35,710baht $1,191 US per month

So even with going crazy every weekend, it's still relatively cheap to eat, sleep, train, and have fun in Thailand. But if you're serious about training and getting in shape, I'd suggest you make a pact to yourself to not go to Patong until the last week before you leave, which is what I did when I trained in Phuket.

Johnny FD

Budget: Training in Chiang Mai

Overall, every day living is cheaper in Chiang Mai than in Phuket. The easiest examples are taxi from the airport to any gym in Phuket would cost you around 600 baht ($20US), vs. any gym in Chiang Mai would only be 150 baht. ($5US) The cost of going to watch a Muay Thai fight in Phuket is 1,200 baht ($40) vs. in Chiang Mai 400 baht ($13US).

Strict Budget - Cheapest Possible per month

Monthly Training - Muay Thai and MMA - 8,000 baht ($266US)

Accommodation: Fan Room with Own Bathroom – 3,500 baht ($116US)
(In Phuket for this price you would have to share a bathroom)

Breakfast – 3 Eggs or Omelet- 20 baht per meal x 30 = 600 baht ($20US)

Lunch - Thai Food - Chicken Basil with Rice, Fried Rice Chicken, Mixed Veggies with Chicken and Rice 40 baht x 30 = 1,200 baht ($40US)

Dinner – Thai Food with a Fried Egg on Top – 45 baht per meal x 30 = 1,350 baht ($45US)

Drinks – Water only. Free at the Gym or 1 baht from a Machine. 56 baht a month ($1.80 US)

Entertainment - Visit one of 40 temples, Hike a really nice mountain, Mountain Biking, sneak into a resorts pool, play board games, watch TV and DVDs, internet - all free.

Total Cost for a Month of Training on a Strict Budget – 14,706 baht - $490 US Dollars.

Compared to Phuket's 20,280 baht - $676US Dollars

*You can save 3,000 baht ($100) by signing up for 1 class a day instead of two, and training on your own on your off time. New total: 11,646 baht or $390US

Obviously, just like Phuket, you'll want some extra nice comforts. The good thing however, everything from massages to taxi fare will be less than half the price of what it would be in Phuket.

Pharmacy - Ibuprofen, Muscle Relaxers, Pain Killers, Muay Thai Liniment Oil, Antibiotic Cream, Tiger Balm, and Re-hydration Powders (powdered Gatorade) 570 baht a month on average. $19US

Motorbike Rental – If you want to go into town everyday or live far from the gym you can rent a bike for around 2,000 baht a month. However, taxi's are so cheap in Chiang Mai that I opted not to get one at all this time around. Instead,

I bought a cheap mountain bike brand new for 2,950 baht ($98US) and pay an average of 10-20 baht per shared taxi ride into town when I want to go. The absolute most you'll pay for taxi is 120 baht even if you hire it privately and need to go way out of town.

Massages – Thai massages in Chiang Mai are often cheaper than in Phuket, they range from 120 baht an hour to 200 baht an hour. $4US - $6.60US)

Movie Theater/Cinema – The movie theater in Chiang Mai is located inside the Airport Plaza Mall where they show new Hollywood movies in English with thai subs, for around 150 baht.

Actual Comfortable Budget per month

Including Training, Accommodation, Food, and Extras – 18,116 baht per month including weekly massages, movies, and a motorbike.

$603 US Dollars.

There isn't a crazy nightlife scene in Chiang Mai as there is in Phuket so you won't be tempted to go out partying on weekends. But there are nice restaurants and some good bars to splurge at, but even then it won't cost you nearly as much as a night in Patong. Expect to add another 800 baht per weekend which would include a nice steak dinner, buffet or Sunday roast, a couple beers with backpackers in town, and maybe even watching a Muay Thai fight. Since Chiang Mai is so cheap to live in, you might as well upgrade your room to one with air conditioning and a view.

Very Comfortable Monthly Budget in Chiang Mai: 22,316 baht a month ($743US) including a nice air conditioned room with refrigerator, TV, and wifi.

Here is an actual excel spreadsheet I made when I first came to Thailand and was living in Koh Tao:

Johnny's Thailand Expenses	BAHT	US$	Notes
Rent – Bungalow	5000	$147	Sairee Beach – Prime Location
Utilities – Water/Electric	1000	$29	
Student Loan – University		$190	Eight more year
Gasoline/Petrol for Motorbike	250	$7	Three tanks per month
Motorbike Maintenance/Repairs	200	$6	Averaged
Mobile Phone	500	$15	Pay as you go

Breakfast Daily	3000	$88	30 meals at 100baht each
Lunch Daily	2400	$71	30 meals at 80 baht each
Mid-Afternoon Snack	1800	$53	30 snacks at 60 baht each
Dinner Daily	3600	$106	30 meals at 120baht each
Drinking Water	450	$13	Bottled and Home Jugs
Coconuts	100	$3	Ten Coconuts
Alcohol/Beer	640	$19	8 drinks at 80baht each
Chocolate	420	$12	12 chocolate bars per month
Snacks	200	$6	Ten snacks at 20 baht each
Fruit	300	$9	Ten shakes or pieces of fruit
Massages	3000	$88	Ten Massages per month
Yoga Classes	1200	$35	1 class per week
Muay Thai Classes	2500	$74	Three classes per week
Scuba Diving	Free	Free	Included in Divemaster
Snorkeling	Free	Free	
Hiking/Trekking	Free	Free	No added expense
Toothpaste/Soap/Shampoo/Etc	300	$9	
Mosquito Repellent	360	$11	Two bottles a month
Sunblock	300	$9	
Tiger Balm	200	$6	
DAN – Diving Insurance	300	$9	Averaged
Clothes – New	600	$18	One to two items a month
Travel – Visa Run or Fun	900	$26	Round trip ferry tickets
Random Hotel Rooms	1000	$29	2-4 nights

Johnny FD

Laundry	350	$10	
Books	500	$15	2 books a month
DVDs	400	$12	1 movie per week
Dog Food	550	$16	1 large bag a month
Visa Cost – Monthly	1000	$29	Averaged
	Baht	US	
Total Monthly Expenses	$39,780	$1,170	
Without Student Loan	$33,320	$980	

As you can see, my costs of living were a bit higher in Koh Tao for a few reasons. First, it's a bit more expensive to live and eat there in general than Chiang Mai, and is on par with living in Phuket. But mainly it was because I had just arrived and wanted to live well and I was eating a lot of western food (as there isn't much good thai food on the island). But mainly the prices are higher because I included every little thing that you often forget you need to factor in.

So whatever budget you are looking at above or Chiang Mai or Phuket, include an extra $100US per month for random stuff that you won't think about, such as your cravings for chocolate or beer. And also factor in another $100 for when your friends come to visit and you go somewhere fun, or when a holiday comes up and you splurge a bit.

Johnny FD

Chapter 3: Making Money while in Thailand

Living as a professional fighter off of your fight purse.

I did a little experiment while living and training with professional fighter named Will "The Kill" Chope. Even though I still had some money in savings at the time, I wanted to see if I could survive off of just my fight purse for month like he does.

First thing, I gave up my normal room at the camp and moved into one of the bamboo huts that are typically reserved only for Thai trainers. I paid Boyd, the owner of the gym 2,500 baht for the month which is $83US. That was exactly half of my winnings of 5,000 baht for the fight. Often if you're actively fighting, and especially if you can get the gym to sponsor you, you won't have to pay nearly as much for training if anything at all. If you ate the cheapest Thai food possible in Phuket, you'll still end up paying around 4,000 baht a month $135US for three meals a day and water.

Johnny and Will Chope in Bangkok at an i-Extreme Magazine Promo

While giving it a shot with Will, I felt seriously impoverished. We would go to the 30 baht Thai buffet and load up, knowing we wouldn't have money to eat much for the rest of the day. At the Thai restaurant, we ordered fried rice everyday as it was the cheapest thing on the menu. (Will liked Kao Pad Saparod, which is pineapple fried rice.) The only time we ever went out was to watch a movie on Wednesday night where it was on special for 80 baht. I ended up going up to Bangkok with him to train at 13 Coins where he was preparing for a fight.

We stayed in the fighter's budget rooms, which was basically the attic above the gym. I've stayed in some low budget rooms in my life, but this was seriously bad. We'd have to climb up an old wooden ladder to get up there, and duck down because you could hardly stand in the room. I had an old mattress with a mosquito net for my bed, and would have to pee out the window at night because it was too dangerous to have to try to climb down the ladder in the dark and walk across the gym into the restaurant to use the bathroom.

As I would close my eyes to go to bed, I heard rodents scurrying around. Worst of all is even on Sundays when I'd try to sleep in, I'd be woken up to music and training at 7am. Luckily Mr. Coke the owner of 13 Coins was such a nice guy, he let me sleep in one of the normal hotel rooms for the remainder of that day. So the question is, is it possible to live off of the fighter's purse in Thailand? The answer is, if you are completely sponsored by the gym, including room and training, then yes, you can scrape by, especially if you fight twice a month. Would it be a nice comfortable life? Nope.

Getting a local job – Tourism, Teacher, Journalist or Guide.
Local Thai's make around 10,000 baht a month ($333US) which is why it's very rare to see a Thai with their own room. The jobs that you could likely get would be as a teacher or a guide. You'll need a TEFL (Teaching English as a Foreign Language) certification, which you can get here in Thailand. The only problem is, you'll work from 8am-5pm which makes you miss both the morning and afternoon Muay Thai class. If you really wanted to, you could take a private afterward and join the normal class on Saturdays but you most likely won't. I recently met a friend at the gym here in KC, Piers from England that doesn't have a TEFL cert and still got a job as an English tutor, so if you're white and speak good English and have a college degree it might not be a strict requirement.

Guides are sought after especially if you speak another language such as Russian, French or Mandarin. I've known some people who picked up side jobs where they take people on tours.

I've met a few journalists out here in Chiang Mai and they work for random international countries that have internet news sites. I made a few friends that work for a Burmese News Station as they are based in Chiang Mai for political reasons. I've also met professional writers here as well.

A more common job would be an underwater guide, a divemaster. Most Thai people don't like swimming and there are very few qualified Thai divemasters, making the majority of workers westerners. I'll talk more about working as a dive guide in chapter 4 and tell you how you can become one in less than 3 months, even if you've never scuba dived before.

Starting your own business in Thailand:

One of the nice things about Thailand is that their unemployment rate is virtually non existent. The reason is because it's so easy for anyone to start a business. You could literally go pick or buy some fruit somewhere, and make a business by selling fresh cut fruit somewhere with a lot of foot traffic. If you wanted to, an easy business that would require nothing more than buying some plastic straws and a butcher knife would be selling ice cold coconuts at the gym after training. They are a fantastic source of electrolytes and very refreshing. But let's take a look at some other businesses first.

Johnny FD

Motorbike Hustler– Make money renting out bikes.

The easiest way to make money in Thailand if you're here long term is to buy a second used motorbike for 10,000 – 15,000 baht and rent it out to people at the gym. You could do so with nothing more than a paper flier on the wall and you could charge 2,500 baht a month and tell the renter that they would just have to pay for whatever damages out of pocket. Within four months your bike will be completely paid off and everything after that will be profit. The best thing is when you go to sell the bike, you'll most likely get 80% - 100% of what you paid for it.

A variation of this idea would be to sell second hand bikes, just make sure you find a good mechanic and fix up the bikes before you sell them for a profit. Labor is ridiculously cheap in Thailand, you'll be surprised how cheap it is to take your bike to the shop.

chia seeds

This "tini" **Superfood** is the **ULTIMATE topping!**

A one ounce serving of Chia Seeds...
- contains 4g of **protein**
- has more **omega-3** fatty acids than salmon
- contains 3x more **calcium** than Skim Milk
- has nearly 11g of **fiber** (42% of your Recommended Daily Value)
- is **gluten free**
- has one of the highest **antioxidant** concentrations of any known food

Top your Yogurtini with Chia Seeds today!

Slanging Chia Seeds – How I paid for my time in Phuket.

I'm going to give you guys the insight and permission to take over my business that I built in Phuket. While in Phuket I read a book "Born to Run" by Christopher McDougall and in it I discovered the health benefits of Chia Seeds, especially for long distance running. I really wanted to try it but couldn't find it anywhere in Thailand. After a lot of searching around, I finally found a source but it was a pain in the ass to get to, literally on top of a mountain at an Elephant camp and I had to order in bulk. So I put up some fliers around the gym, Phuket Top Team and Tiger Muay Thai as well as Tony's restaurant, with Chia Seeds for sale.

Johnny FD

I was surprised how many people wanted them. I guess it made sense, people training are always looking for healthy things. What made me really like Chia seeds was I could just add a teaspoon to my water, let it soak for 20 minutes and all the sudden, I had a drink that kept me full, and gave me enough energy to get through my run and Muay Thai workout without having to eat anything in the morning.

I sold it for 500 baht ($16.60) for a 300 gram bag which is about 10 ounces. You can either bring a bunch with you from home or buy it in bulk in Phuket. If you plan on bringing a lot, you might want to check with customs first to see if it's okay, since it's a seed and all. My source in Phuket is called Good Karma and their website is www.healthfoodthailand.com

If you buy it in bulk, 2 kilos is 1,955 baht and you can order it online and pick it up locally at:

Sunshine Coffee Shop in Kata Noi - Order online and pick up the next day (except Thursday).Open daily from 10am-5pm

Book Cafe Phuket in Nai Harn - order online and pick up in 2 business days. Open Tues - Sat 10am-6pm

If you do the math, if you buy 4 kilos for 3,910 baht ($130US) and sell the thirteen 300 gram portions for 500 baht a piece, your gross sales will be 6,500 baht ($216US) which is a pretty decent profit for not doing much. The funny thing was, I felt kind of like a drug dealer when I was slangin' chia seeds. I'd have guys randomly drop by my room and ask for a bag, then ask me to show them how to use it before they left. I got calls on my local cell phone and even people asking for me at restaurants I'd frequently be at. At the end of the day, it was an easy business with almost no up front cost (the first order I actually collected cash up front before I went to buy it.) and it's something that is actually healthy and useful, the exact opposite of selling dope.

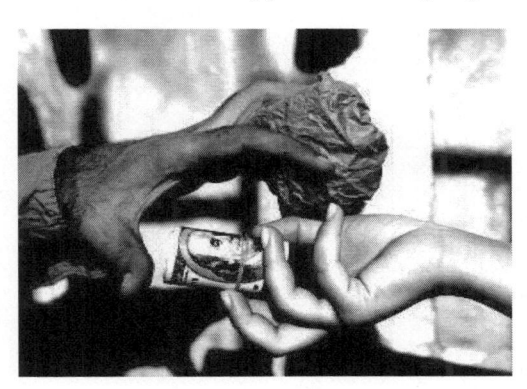

Restaurant idea – Start it for under a hundred bucks.

My friend Sonic wanted to move from California back to his home town Indianapolis, Indiana to open a taco restaurant since they didn't really have any good ones there.

I told him it was a terrible idea, and that 1 in 4 restaurants fail within the first year. But I knew he was really excited about the idea, so I suggested to him to instead, open a temporary ad hoc restaurant on the street in front of the building they were looking to lease. That way they could really see how many people they could expect to walk by on any given day and if they did well with their temporary food stall, then they would know the restaurant itself would do well. On the flip side, if there wasn't enough customers, they wouldn't have lost much money.

They took that idea and opened a mobile food truck instead, called West Coast Tacos, which was the very first food truck in the city when they first opened. It was an instant success and they were even all over the news for it. He sold his share a year later and now successfully owns a pizza truck called the NY Slice as well as a brand new nightclub.

In Thailand, it's even easier to start a small restaurant. The nice thing about Thailand is you can start a business anywhere, literally in front of your house. However, if you start making money, then it gets really complicated really fast especially if you're not Thai. I would suggest to not open a real restaurant or invest any money in opening a business until you have a Thai partner. Even then, I heard stories all of the time about guys getting screwed out of their money from their Thai partners which legally own everything, so I personally wouldn't do it. If you want to open a little food stand however, it'll be easy, cheap to start up and a great way to make a bit of cash. Think rotisserie chicken stand or taco stand.

Making money online – Blogs, eBooks and Internet Marketing.
Making money online is the best choice for topping up your funds for long term travel. However, it's also the one that takes the longest to start up and requires the most amount of technical skills. I'll try to show you the basics how to do it without knowledge of making websites or anything too complicated. Best of all, everything I'm going to show you won't cost more than $20 to get started.
For me, this book started with a personal blog that I never intended to make money from. I started it just for fun, and it turned out to be an important source of information for people wanting to come to Thailand to train Muay Thai and MMA. I didn't even realize there was such demand or lack of information for traveling and this new genre I refer to as, "sports tourism." Hopefully your passion will become your next source of income.

The first step is to start a free blog
Use blogger.com also known as blogspot.com to get started. Both of which are the same and powered by google. The other option would be wordpress.com which is much more complicated for beginners but is more powerful and lets you do some things blogger won't in the long run. The biggest benefit of starting a blog is that you can start it today and learn the skills behind making websites.

I opted to go with blogger and don't have any regrets. The idea of the blog is to write about something you genuinely enjoy writing about and want to share with others. For me, it was my passion of muay thai but also the enjoyment of traveling to different gyms and checking them out. Find your passion and write about it, and remember, the more niche the better. In an age where there is so much information out there, you will never stick out trying to write about something too general. A Martial Arts website that talks about everything from Taekwondo in Korean to Boxing in America won't build an audience like a website dedicated to one martial art in a single place, such as boxing gyms in the Philippines or in my case, Muay Thai in Thailand.

My friend's mother started a successful blog about feeding her cats a raw meat diet. Another successful website is one that reviews old style razor blades and shaving cream brushes made from badger hair. Think as niche as possible and try to have it be something personal, and something that not many other people are already writing about. So unfortunately unless you started writing your Muay Thai blog about Thailand 3 years ago, you'll have a lot of catching up to do. However, if you wrote a Muay Thai blog about gyms in the Philippines or in the Netherlands, you'll be an instant success as no one else is in that market yet.

The trick is to find a topic that you personally are interested in, something that even if you never made a cent from, you would continue to do it. Chances are, if you are interested it in, others will be as well. If you don't believe me, look up random things that you didn't think would exist like a blog about not being able to fall asleep unless you have a plugged in hairdryer with you in bed, they exist.

Step 2: Get visitors
The easiest way to get traffic to your blog is to write about your experiences and keep it personal. Make it so your friends will want to read it, and strangers will start to feel like they are getting to know the author. When writing posts, follow the same format that I do on my blog, always have at least one or two photos with each post, and don't make them too long. Try to stay away from stock photos, use ones that you took yourself whenever possible. Videos are a great way to engage readers as well, but just like photos, they are much better if it is original content.

The three places you'll get the most amount of traffic is facebook, google, and links. The first step is to simply link your blog on your facebook. I put up a link on my personal facebook whenever I write a new article. You can also email your friends and tell them about your new blog.

Second you'll want to try to get your blog linked from other websites. The easiest way is to have it in your signature box when you post on forums related to your subject. You can also have your website linked to comments on leave on other people's blogs, try to keep it all relevant to your topic.

The last way to get traffic is through google. The way google ranks how relevant your blog is and how high it should be on the search page is by how good your content is, don't try to trick google, it doesn't work. Instead, write about topics that people would be interested in. For Muay Thai, people often search for topics like gym reviews, and food costs. The trick is, if you're the first, or only one writing about a topic, you'll be #1 on the google search, so that's why it's a good idea to keep it as niche as possible. The only reason why my blog ranks so high on google searches is because I was one of the first. I started keeping my Muay Thai blog a few years ago before many other people had one, and I was the first to write a lot of gym reviews. I also got a lot of links from other websites for putting up good, original content like my "Actual cost of living breakdown" that a lot of people share on their websites as well.

Here are my blog's actual statistics, something that website owners usually keep confidential. But I'm sharing it because it's a good way to show you exactly what I'm talking about. First you have the graph of how many page views I get a day, today I've gotten 144 so far, but it's only lunch time so that's not a very good indicator. A better indicator is how many I got yesterday which was 303, as that's an entire 24 hour period. 303 page views doesn't mean 303 visitors, as a single visitor might have went through older posts or clicked around my site and looked at 3 or 4 pages before he left. However, these are the types of visitors you want.

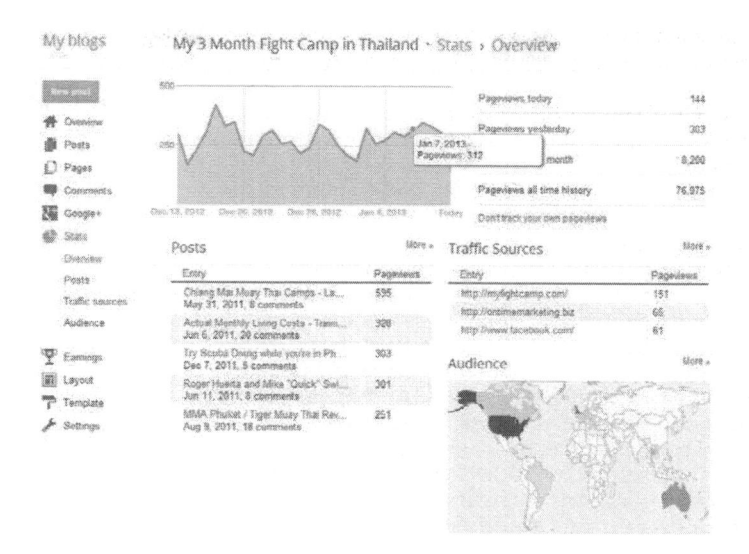

If you have 1,000 visitors but they all leave right away, or leave after looking at the first place, you don't have a successful website. You want at least an average of 2.3 pages per visitor and an average time of at least 3 minutes on your site. This means the majority of your visitors stay long enough to read your front page, but also click and read more. The nice thing about blogger/blogspot is that it has a page view counter and basic statistics built in. One suggestion I have however, is even though you won't be using it for the first few months as it's overly complicated, it's a good idea to have google start tracking your website's performance from day one, using the powerful, google analytics tracker.

It's free to set up, but pretty complicated to use, so I suggest, set it up, and forget about it until you actually need it a year from now. The good news is, once you sign up for an account, all you have to do with blogger is copy and paste a tracker code into your account, you can have someone do this for you if it seems to complicated. Set it, then forget it, and just use the much simpler one that comes built in with blogger.

Step 3: Keeping in touch with visitors

Your goal is to keep each visitor coming back to your website. There's no point of getting 1,000 people to visit your page once if they never come back again, especially since you won't be selling anything for the first few months or even the first year. First and foremost, you need to give people a reason to want to come back, you need to update your blog regularly and have good content. Second, you need a way to remind people to come back or to let them know when you update.

Johnny FD

The old school way to keep in touch with visitors is getting them to sign up for your mailing list. It's still a good idea to collect email addresses and send them updates directly, but it's not cheap. I use aweber, which is the best, but it's not worth the money for most people. Instead, start with a free service such as mailchimp.com, listwire.com, or imnicamail.com

The more up to date way to keep in touch with visitors is through facebook. You have two options, the first is to create a fan page, and the second is to use a personal facebook page. The personal page is easier to add friends, and get started with, and is all around better, the only downside is there is an upper limit maximum of 5,000 friends. I would suggest you start a separate, personal facebook for your interest/blog/website and then start a fan page when you get to 5,000. Don't be tempted to use your personal facebook as you'll end up having so many random people added that you won't feel comfortable sharing normal pictures or info and your real life friends will hate you.

The problem with creating a fan page is it's harder to interact with others and leave comments or send messages to people. It's more limited since it's a business. You also can't add people as friends, you have to get them to "like" you. So unless you plan on paying for facebook advertising, there is no upside to creating a fan page, which is something I learned the hard way. It's a ten times easier to get 500 friends on facebook than it is to get 500 likes on your fan page. It's also more likely for someone to "unlike" your page than it is for them to unfriend you.

Step 4: Creating and Selling a Product

The easiest product to create and sell is an eBook. You can also turn it into a hard copy book through self publishing with sites such as lulu.com however, the downside is that it'll cost you up to $20 a book to print and ship since you'll be doing it low quantities. With eBook readers such as the Kindle becoming cheap and widely available, eBooks are they way to go for self publishing.

The content itself should be easy, if you've been updating your blog for quite sometime now, you'll already have plenty of content. Now you just need to put it in a logical order and expand on it. You'll know which topics people have the most questions about from the comments they leave you. For this book, I simply wrote an introduction, created a table of contents, which was an outline of what I wanted to talk about then expanded in deeper detail on things that I've already talked about on my blog. Even though people could technically have read my entire blog from start to finish and pieced it all together to get 80% of what's in this book, it's worth it to people to have all the information in one place in an easy to follow format. Plus I get to update and go into much more detail in the book than on my blog, especially with things that I didn't want to publicly talk about on my blog.

The main idea of your product is that it needs to address some type of unfulfilled need. The best way to figure out what that problem is, is to read and respond to comments people leave on your blog. You will soon notice a trend on people's fears and needs. That'll be your product.

The trick to writing a book is to force yourself to sit down and write at least two pages a day. You'll often write more, but if you don't, weeks will go by where it'll be untouched with no progress. So two pages a day, simple. Another little program that has helped me tremendously is a timer called workrave. It's free and it's just a little sheep on my computer that knows if I've been on it for too long and need a break. I set mine for a 3 minute break every 45 minutes. I end up being much more productive with it because it gives me a chance to walk around, get some water, shadow box, get some air, use the bathroom and come back and go straight back to work. Often when my break comes up I'll be in the middle of doing something unproductive like searching the internet. It'll cut me off and remind me to not waste hours on non productive things. Studies have also shown that it's incredibly bad for your body to sit for hours at a time. Once your book is finished, use E-Junkie which is the company I used to sell this book. It only costs $5 a month and is really easy to use. They even have an ebook called "Publishing Your First eBook" that you can download for free. You can also sell your book through Amazon's Kindle Store, but they take 30% and it's a bit limited as not everyone in the world has a kindle or kindle program.

Make Money by Recommending this Book to Others

An easy way to start making money in the meantime is to help other people spread the word on products you believe in through affiliate marketing. Basically, anytime you buy something and find it useful, put up a link and recommend it to your friends and family either through facebook, email or on your blog. It's easier than you think, and as long as you only recommend things you truly believe in then it's mutually beneficial to everyone involved. For an example, you obviously liked the idea of this book enough to buy it for yourself, so why not recommend it to your friends that have similar interests to you? They'll be happy you did, I'll be happy you did, and you'll end up making some extra cash from it. Most retailers such as Amazon.com will give you anywhere between 4%-8% of sales.

Give it a shot, sign up here to become an affiliate then simply put a link in your facebook status saying that you bought this book and recommend it. See what happens, you might be pleasantly surprised on how easy it is. Sign up as an Amazon affiliate by going to affiliate-program.amazon.com.

It'll give you a code that you can copy and paste into your website or blog and paste it into your facebook status along with,

"Hey guys check out this book I just read" the link will redirect anyone that clicks on it to my blog, and if they buy a book, you'll automatically get a percentage of the sale. It takes a minute to figure out the first time, but it's actually really easy once you get the hang of it. After the initial facebook status, which is the easiest thing you can do. You can write a review of the book on your blog or website and include your affiliate link there as well. Basically, anytime someone clicks your affiliate link and later buys the book, you'll get paid. Reviews are good because it gives the reader deeper reason why you bought it and why they should buy it as well. You can say things like,

"I bought this book because I've been following Johnny's blog for a while now and it's been super helpful in planning my trip to Thailand to train Muay Thai. It's written

really well and has so much more information in it than his blog. If you are planning a trip to Thailand to train or even just to live vicariously through his life, buy this book, it's worth every penny."

Then obviously include your unique link. The cool thing is, even if they don't buy the book that day, and come back a week later, you'll still get credit for it. Give it a shot. Even if you don't need the money now, it's good to start building a way to generate passive income, so when you do start traveling, you'll have money coming in without even working!

Make money on quick gigs, one at a time online:

There's a website called Fiverr.com where you can make $5 at a time for whatever random skill you have. Easy popular ones are video testimonials for products. You'll get a 75 word script saying, "Check out the new Pepsi Diet! It's so refreshing I can't believe it!" There are also little gigs for creating logos, ebook covers, proof reading, voice overs, graphic design, transcriptions, photo touch up, video editing, drawing, signing, dancing, movie star impersonations, almost everything. It's not a lot of money per gig, but it adds up and it's something that you can easily do while traveling. A lot of it is as easy as taking a photo of you holding up a sign for their business or writing a review.

I made the cover of this book using fiverr, I paid someone $15 to do the whole thing and it was well worth my time instead of trying to figure out photoshop and design it myself. The intial price was $5, but I added on two additional options making it a decent pay day for someone who already knows how to design covers. It also works well for people with random internet skills as you can queue them up and do 20 at once, really only working a few days a week.

Make $80 an Hour While Traveling:
If you have more specialized skills such as web design, programming, graphic design, podcast editing, language translation, etc you can accept gigs on Odesk.com or FreeLancer.com

*At the time of writing this book I was still relatively new to online business. Check out my blog www.JohnnyFD.com for the latest updates. Now I make money with an online retail store, based in the U.S., selling to U.S. Customers, but I'm able to manage it from wherever I am in the world. I started the business in my last few months in Thailand and since everything is outsourced, drop shipped and automated, I am able to travel and make money from anywhere.

If you are interested in how to build an online business using drop shipping, check out my post, "Start Here" which is on the right hand side of my blog.

Johnny FD

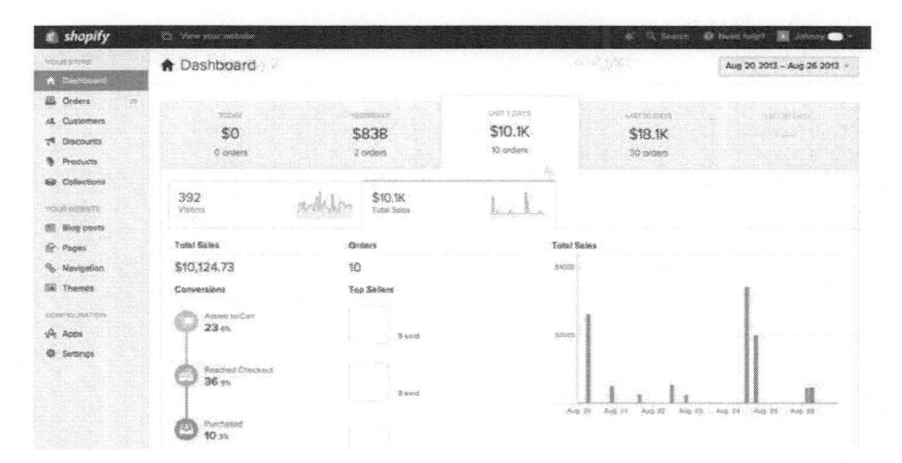

Here is a screen shot from my first months of sales after getting the store up and running. Keep in mind, I did all this while living in Chiang Mai on a borrowed laptop!

Chapter 4: Life as a Divemaster turned Scuba Instructor

Before discovering Muay Thai, I discovered scuba diving, literally I took a one day trial dive and ended up loving it. After completing my open water certification, which is the basic 3 day class, I decided then and there that I wanted to move to Thailand and work as a Divemaster.

Initially, I had no money saved up, so I sold my car. With the $8,000 I received from it, I figured I could pay for a flight back to Thailand, complete the dive master course, and start making money while traveling. I admit, I was super naïve about the whole thing, but somehow it all worked itself out. Hopefully you can learn from some of my mistakes and have a clearly idea of what you're getting yourself into if you decide to go this route.

I did my basic courses in Phuket, but decided to go to Koh Tao to do the rest. Good thing I did, as it turns out Koh Tao is a hell of a lot cheaper to live and get certified. Mainly I wanted to get away from the craziness of Phuket and the idea of living on a simpler, smaller island had it's charms. I arrived in November, which turns out is the one month you shouldn't go to Koh Tao due to the monsoon. But I did end up finding a nice bungalow and a used motorbike for cheap because it was the slow season. I paid 5,000 baht a month at a place called Sairee Cottage which is on the main beach of Koh Tao. My hut was further back from the beach, across the main road in a coconut plantation. There were three dogs there that belonged to a French girl that went home, I quickly adopted them and named them Pepsi, Cola and Scruffy.

Johnny FD

Thinking back and reminiscing, I really had an amazing time that first trip to Koh Tao. Like all places, you eventually find things you don't like about it and want to move on, but I truly was happy those first 6 months on that island. There are literally 50+ dive shops on the island, but I ended up going with Scuba-Junction, a small shop in the middle of Sairee Beach. I walked in and told them I wanted to become a Dive Master, they were surprised when I told them I had only been diving 4 times in my life and hadn't even done the Advanced Open Water class yet, which is the second step. Talk about jumping feet first into the water! But I did it, I did my AOW class, then my Rescue Diver Class including CPR/Emergency First Responder. Finally I got to start my Dive Master training.

I was luckily to have an instructor by the name of Jez, a Turkish military guy that really cared and knew what he was doing. I have him to thank for training me to be as good underwater as I am today. I took my sweet time finishing the course and ended up traveling a bit and going back to the U.S. for a month during it. I honestly think that trying to rush it, going from never been diving before to being a Divemaster in 2 months is crazy and although it's possible, you won't be comfortable even after you get your DM. To complete your dive master course, you need to do a bunch of classroom and theory, including Physics of Diving, Physiology of your body and how it reacts to scuba diving, Decompression theory and a bunch of other things. Luckily for you, as of last year, PADI, the world's largest certification company (think Visa or Mastercard) revised the Divemaster program and make it a lot less theory heavy.

You'll still need to complete the DM swim tests which are timed tests including 15 minute treading water, 400m swim (no gear), 800m snorkel (masks, fins, and snorkel), and a 100m tired diver tow (both in full scuba). Then there's some tests in scuba gear itself, all which were really fun now that I think back on it, although it was quite stressful when you're the one being graded.

Immediately after my training finished, Natalie, the owner of Scuba Junction offered me a job. I was nervous at first, but quickly got the hang of taking certified divers underwater with me and showing them around. Working as a Divemaster was seriously one of the best jobs I've ever had. It was fun, relatively stress free, as the divers were already certified and supposedly knew what they were doing. At the time I had my complaints of difficult customers and hard days, but it wasn't until became a Scuba Instructor did I realize how easy I had it. But more on that later.

In search of better diving, I moved to Koh Lanta and wow, it was seriously much better. The water was clearer, there was a million times better marine life and since the boat rides were much longer, you were never in a rush. I'd still recommend doing your dive master course in Koh Tao though as it's literally half the price. Just make sure you stay there and get some work experience before coming to Koh Lanta.

One thing they don't tell you when doing your dive master course is how difficult it will be to get a job after you're done. Basically there are only three ways to get a job as an inexperienced DM, the first is get hired by the same company that trained you, which is likely because they know your experience and personality first hand. The second is if you speak a language they desperately need, such as French, German, Russian, Mandarin, and sometimes Swedish. Third is to get lucky. Seriously. Sometimes you just need to be at the right place at the right time. Luckily, I've figured out when and where that is. If you want a dive master job in Koh Tao, show up at the shops you want a job around 4-5pm the days after the full moon.

There's a huge party every month on the neighboring island, Koh Phangan and it's part of the tourist route to party there, and then go to Koh Tao to chill out and learn to scuba dive after. The reason why 4pm is a good time to go is often the shop will have too many customers and not enough guides by that time and they'll need to call someone to work freelance. Be flexible, even if they only give you one customer, if that's the shop you want to work for, do it with a smile and soon they'll hire you full time.

Johnny FD

Becoming a Scuba Instructor: Why it may kill your passion for diving.

I decided to take the next step after Dive Master and become a full on scuba instructor mainly because I love teaching and second it seemed like as a DM I had to do all of the grunt work, like carrying scuba tanks, while they just joked around with their students. You also get paid hell of a lot more as an instructor verses being a DM. What no one told me was that going through the process of becoming an instructor, you start to see the business side of the dive training industry and often get a really bad taste in your mouth from it.

The big dive certification companies are geniuses at marketing and getting people to try and fall in love with scuba diving. The problem is that they try to convince every diver to go through their entire training program, all the way up to instructor. There simply aren't enough jobs in the world to support that many professionals. What really saddens me is how many people invest their savings into the program, get certified as an instructor, and go home because they can't find a job. They lose their passion for diving, and become jaded. The truth is, most big dive centers that offer Instructor Development Courses are only physically capable of hiring 3% of their students afterward, even as a non-paid intern.

I would recommend to most people to work as a Divemaster for at least 3 years before you even think about becoming an instructor. It's not worth the extra money and stress. Do not be scammed into thinking that as an instructor you will be able to find work easier, if you cannot find a job as a paid DM, you will not find a job as an instructor.

If you still want to do your instructor course, I would recommend you do it at a small to medium sized dive center, and get in writing through email that you will be allowed to stay after the course. Tell them that you are happy to work for free, but want the experience. Do not pay to be an internship, or an MSDT internship, which is the next ranking up. You can find it included for free if you look around and I feel like it should be part of the program anyway since you don't actually learn how to teach a course during your IDC. You'll be paying close to $3,000US after you add up all of the PADI fees, textbooks, equipment pack, and random things that you won't be aware of until you are committed. Don't be fooled into thinking it'll only be $1,000, trust me, it's not.

I know Crystal Dive Resort in Koh Tao will let you help out on a few courses for free after your IDC (instructor development course) finishes but email them and find out exactly how many you can sit through. Lanta Divers in Koh Lanta, and maybe some dive centers in Phuket may let you work as a non-paid intern after your class. Don't be afraid to ask around first, and don't fall into the hype of "Best IDC Course Director." To be honest, none of that matters, you can do your IDC at the best IDC center in the world with the best course director and you still won't know anything about teaching a class until you shadow someone afterward and then actually do it yourself. You're basically paying for nothing more than a certification and knowledge of the company's standards.
The only two ways to get a job as a dive instructor after your IDC program is either to speak a language that is desperately needed, such as French, German, Chinese, Japanese, Korean, Russian and maybe a few others such as Dutch or

Swedish depending on where you are. The second way to get a job as a new, inexperienced instructor is through relationships. You can either do this by doing your IDC at the same place you worked as a dive master, or you can do your IDC somewhere where they will guarantee you a free internship afterward and hope that will turn into a paid job. Most English instructors who don't speak a second language end up working at the same dive company for years as they know it'll be hard for them to find another job else where.
A bit outside of Thailand is the best company I've ever worked for. It's out of the way, but once you are there, it's quite cheap to live and aside from the massive garbage problem which I sincerely hope they educate and enforce the locals about soon, it's the most amazing diving I've ever seen. In Koh Tao, you may see 1 turtle a month if you are lucky. In Koh Lanta you may see one a day, on a good day. On Mabul you will see an average of 6 per dive. I highly recommend Scuba-Junkie in Mabul, Malaysia as the best dive resort I've personally been to in terms of Dive Master training, Instructor training and working there. The only reason why I am no longer in Borneo where Scuba-Junkie is located is because they don't have Muay Thai which is my first passion. Secondly, the litter in the water really put me off, almost to a point where it disgusts me. I would still highly recommend it for your Divemaster and Instructor courses.
I personally ended up doing my instructor's course at Utila Dive Center in Honduras. Having been in Thailand for almost two years at that point, I was looking for somewhere better, hoping the water would be bluer on the other side of the world. The reason why I do not recommend Utila or the surrounding islands is because there are not nearly enough job opportunities for dive instructors. From my calculations less than 3% of instructors find a paying job there. Even though Koh Tao is known to have too many instructors as well, if you wait around until after the full moon party every month, you'll at least be able to free lance somewhere and get your foot in the door. If you speak another language that is needed, you will eventually find a job there or in Koh Phi Phi. On Utila, that's simply not the case.

I did however learn a very valuable lesson from the process of spending the rest of my savings venturing across the globe that almost made it worth it. I learned to appreciate Thailand 1,000x more and realized that I need to be happy where I am instead of hoping the grass is greener on the other side. It's not. Thailand is an amazing place, and so is most of South East Asia. It's much cheaper than other parts in the world as well.
Just remember, that unless you speak a second language, your chances of finding work as an inexperienced DM or Instructor is almost zero, which is why it is vital to stay and work at the shop you trained at for at least 3 - 6 months after your course. Before signing up for a course, make sure they promise you at minimum a non-paid internship until you can find a paid job. If they cannot, look else where, trust me, this is non-negotiable. Don't think for a second that just because you are a good person and work hard that they will hire you, some places in the world just don't have the need for you.

Moving back to Koh Tao:
After spending half a year and most of my savings on my regretful journey to Utila, I moved back to Koh Tao attempting to look for a job there as an instructor. Without any work experience and a flood of new instructors on the island (Koh Tao is another place where they train way too many instructors for the amount of

jobs in the area) I had a really difficult time getting my foot in the door anywhere. Three weeks later, I finally got an opportunity at Crystal Dive Resort in Mae Haad which is the port town area of the island.
Turns out my second language saved my dive career, and if it wasn't for the fact that I spoke Mandarin Chinese, I never would have gotten a job since I didn't have any work experience as an instructor. I shadowed another instructor and completed a free non-paid internship before getting students of my own. I worked there for around 4 months before I got burnt out dealing with students from mainland China that would often show up unprepared, uncomfortable in the water and not knowing how to swim.

My second language was both a blessing and a curse, it got me a job and free training, and I got to improve my Chinese by teaching diving in it. However, the problem with Chinese divers is that most never learned how to swim as a kid and are uncomfortable in the water. The second problem is due to clever marketing and word of mouth they come on vacation looking to scuba dive but don't realize how much hard work it really is. Most instructors and dive centers will squeeze them through the course somehow but it's a very stressful process. My advice would be to only work for dive shops that make it very clear to all divers that book in advance, especially anyone from Asian countries that they must first go to a local swimming pool and pass the swim tests on their own before they come. That way, they'll be comfortable in the water and ready to learn.

The Best place to do Muay Thai and work as a Scuba Diver:
Phuket would seem like a good choice because there are excellent Muay Thai gyms, as well as really good scuba diving. Unfortunately, Phuket is the hardest place in Thailand to get a dive job. No where else in the country do they make you get a work permit, which is a pain in the ass and a complicated legal process. The other problem is the big dive shops are all the way in Patong Beach which is a 40 minute drive from Chalong where Tiger Muay Thai, Phuket Top Team and most gyms are located. It wouldn't be realistic to drive back and forth, especially with all of your scuba gear. If you were really serious about giving it a try, you might get lucky, but don't expect it to be easy.

I would have loved Koh Tao to have good Muay Thai, as the island itself has a good hiking trail, a lot of dive shops to work at, and a good overall lifestyle for the money there. Unfortunately, as you'll read later, Koh Tao has the worst Muay Thai gym I've ever trained at.

Koh Phangan and Koh Samui are neighboring islands with better Muay Thai gyms, especially Koh Samui, however, due to over development of land, the beach sand has completely covered all of the island's surrounding coral and there is no longer any scuba diving around the islands. There is one dive site half way between Koh Phangan and Koh Tao called Sail Rock which is very good but too advanced and deep for beginners. Aside from that, you would have to go to Koh Tao to dive. Thailand really fucked up their reefs and fish life by over fishing and over developing their beach front properties. By clearing all the trees and building up the coast, sand washes into the sea covering the coral. Fifty years ago there were beautiful coral reefs surrounding the islands, and now there is just sand.

However, it would be possible to live and train in Koh Phangan or Koh Samui and scuba dive part time. It's not ideal to work full time in diving and train, but if you're just doing it free lance or part time it would work out.
Pattaya has terrible diving conditions. The water is murky and the visibility is bad. There is decent Muay Thai there but a really seedy quality of life, it's the one place in Thailand I refuse to go.

Koh Lanta would be the only ideal place to do Muay Thai and work in Scuba Diving full time. The Muay Thai gym is called Koh Lanta Muay Thai and the owner, William, also owns the Muay Thai stadium. It's not the best Muay Thai training in Thailand mainly because there is no competition on the island with other gyms. The trainers also don't care too much about you or love Muay Thai as passionately as gyms in Chiang Mai would. But overall, decent Muay Thai training, rooms at the camp itself, and easy access to fighting in the stadium. The diving in Koh Lanta is the best in Thailand with the Similans competing for the #1 spot. The only downside is that unless you speak Swedish, French or German it may be very difficult to find a diving job there. The diving season starts in the beginning of November and most shops hire through email a month before hand so make sure you send in your CV or Resume early and state your languages.

The only other downside of Koh Lanta is that it has a very short diving season, from December until February. With one or two months before and afterward open as well. For the other half of the year, the island is abandoned, and since tourists mainly come for the diving, I doubt there are any stadium fights during those months either.

Where to go and when:
If I wanted to train Muay Thai full time and just go for a fun dive one a month, I would do it in Phuket. If I was going to combine working in diving and muay thai, I would spend November – April in Koh Lanta and spend the rest of the year in Koh Phangan or Koh Samui.

For beginners I would do my discover scuba dive introduction and my open water certification in either Koh Lanta or Phuket. It's a bit more expensive than it is in Koh Tao but I personally think the experience is worth it. I did my first dives in Phuket and fell in love immediately. The non-rushed long boat rides on the way there and on the way back, plus lunch and drinks on the boat make it all that much more special. Who knows if I would have fell in love with diving if I had done it somewhere else.

For doing your advanced open water, rescue diver and dive master course I would recommend doing it in either Koh Phi Phi or Koh Tao. It's a lot cheaper and you will have a good chance of landing a job on the island afterward. Just remember before you do your divemaster course, ask if you can work as a non-paid dive master for a month afterward and see what they say. I would continue to look around until someone says yes.

Relationships, Dating and Hooking up:
In the beginning of my new found life living in Koh Tao, I decided to go check out the legendary full moon party at the neighboring island of Koh Phangan.

How to get to the Full Moon Party:
The ferry ride over from Koh Tao was around 1.5 hours and cost around 400 baht ($13.50), there are three different ferry services with different prices and speeds, just find one that fits your schedule. Once on Koh Phangan you are dropped off at Thong Sala which is the main port town of the island. You'll need to hop on a shared taxi and pay the flat 100 baht ($3.33US) fee to get to Haad Rin beach, which is about 30 minutes away where the actual party is held.

Unless you are just coming for the night and don't plan to sleep, (bad idea, I've tried it once) you must come a few days early to get a hotel as most places get booked up in advance. I stayed at a small hotel called Oasis near Mr. K's chicken corner for around 1,000 baht a night ($33US). On another visit, I splurged with a friend and got a room at the Phangan Sunrise Resort which is right on the beach in the middle of the party. (3,000 baht a night/$100US) Also on the luxury end of the price scale is Palita Lodge which is the best place I've stayed on the island. Just to mix it up, I've also stayed at the Dancing Elephant Hostel as well. All hotels now make you book 5 nights during the full moon party period. Ironically, if you came a few weeks in advance, you could find a place for the entire month for around the same price.

My first night of the party:
There's a running joke that the first girl you'll hook up with in Thailand is going to be from England. In my case she was. We met on the beach while dancing, both pretty intoxicated, and ended up sneaking off behind a rock together. To be honest, I don't remember much else from that night, as most people don't. It's truly one of the last hedonistic places left on earth where you can go, let loose, drink to your hearts content and hook up on the beach or even in the sea.

By the way, what most people don't know is that the first night of the full moon party, actually starts three nights before and is much more fun than the night itself. On the night of the actual full moon, people arrive from Koh Samui for just the night, with name tags around their neck, buddy checks to make sure no one gets lost and other precautions. The beach is overcrowded and if you lose your friends, it's almost impossible to find them again.

Even though the party is at full swing on the actual night of the full moon, no one has as much fun as they do on the two nights leading up to it Trust me on this, if you're going to the FMP, go three days before the listed date. It's the same party, same beach, same DJs, it'll just be less crowded and people will be letting loose and having more fun. You'll be able to hook up with someone and still find your friends afterward. It's a win win situation. I'd almost consider partying the nights before and skipping the actual full moon party itself.

The Thai Girl and the Pickpocket:
During the night of the Full Moon Party, there were over 10,000 people dancing away on the beach. We all had a bucket of liquor, which was literally a sand pail filled with ice a flask of whiskey and a red bull topped with coke and a lime. I

had gone through about three of these by that time as most people have by midnight. While walking through the crowd a skimpy dressed Thai girl touches my chest and starts dancing with me, it takes me a minute or two to realize that she's no girl at all, but instead a lady boy. I quickly walk away, only to realize moments later that she had taken my wallet. That was my first and last experience ever with a lady boy in the three years I've now been in Thailand. But I was left with no money for the night and no way home.

I met another Thai girl later that night, a real girl this time. The funny thing is if a girl looks really plain, is short, and not dressed very sexy, she's most likely a real girl. But if the "girl" is tall, wearing a lot of makeup, with her hair and nails done, and wearing something revealing, she's most likely not a she at all, just a really convincing lady boy.

I was a bit hesitant with this new girl, but as I had no money left to steal anyway, I had nothing to loose. We hung out and danced for a bit when she asked if I was hungry and wanted to get something to eat. I told her yeah sure, but then remembered I didn't have even a single dollar on me. I told her what happened and that I got my wallet stolen and she told me not to worry and that it was her treat.

We sat down at a local Thai restaurant and I had some chicken fried rice, but the entire time I was paranoid. I was afraid that she had drugged my food. When she asked what hotel I was staying at and offered to come home with me, I really freaked out, I was suspicious of everyone, especially of Thai women. But I had nothing to lose and no money left, so I took her home, double bolted the door had and thought for sure she would be the last person I would have have sex with as I would wake up in a bathtub full of ice with a kidney missing.

But nothing happened. We woke up in an embrace, the crazy night had ended, but I still had no way back to my island. Then I had a brilliant idea, I asked her if she wanted to come hang out with me in Koh Tao for a couple days. I told her that she could stay with me and I'd pay her back as soon as we got home. She let me borrow a 1,000 baht to pay for breakfast and the ferry ride back and it was then that I finally let my guard down and realized she wasn't trying to sell my organs on the black market.

Back in Koh Tao, we spend the first night in my room, the bamboo hut in the middle of a coconut plantation. Aside from going out to eat, we mainly hung out in the room. The next day, I asked if she wanted to go explore the island, hang out on the beach, go snorkeling, hiking, whatever she wanted, but she insisted on laying around the hut once again. By the third day, she didn't even want to go out to eat, she wanted to build me a kitchen so she could cook for me at home. I know some guys would love that, a nice girl that you would cook and clean for you, where you'd never have to spend money and take her out anywhere, you could just stay home watch tv, have sex and eat. I suddenly realized I had somehow ended up with a live in Thai girlfriend. The next morning I gave her 1,000 baht, put her on a ferry back to her island and said good bye. But she wouldn't be my last accidental Thai girlfriend.

Dating a Thai girl:
There are two types of Thai girls, the first is the one that you will never meet at a bar, the really traditional Thai girls, ones that come from wealthy families, have good jobs and went to college. These are the girls that most guys convince themselves they have, but in reality they have a bar girl, which I'll talk about in a second.

I've only dated one traditional Thai girl. I was introduced to her through the translator I hired to take me to Wat Bang Phra, the Tattoo Temple outside of Bangkok where you can get traditional tattoos done by a monk. We had gotten along really well and he asked me what I had planned for that evening. I had no idea it was valentine's day and had no plans, so when he offered to set up a dinner date for me I accepted. Her name was Ami and she was a nice traditional Thai girl currently in graduate school getting her masters degree. She spoke decent English and was quite pleasant to hang out with.

We had dinner at a place called Coffee Beans by Dao, which had really good food and incredible cakes. We went for a walk afterward, I tried to hold her hand and she freaks out. At the end of the night I go to kiss her cheek and she freaked out again. So I assumed she just wasn't into me and called it a night. I wasn't too bothered but was really surprised when she called me again the next day wanting to hang out. This time we just had coffee and cake at a hotel bar, really romantic place but again even a hug was out of the question. I was really confused and just assumed she wanted to be friends and I was okay with that. But for exactly one year afterward she would call, email and basically act like she was my girlfriend, a girl that I've never even kissed at this point. It turns out that traditional Thai girls are like other Asian girls where they are extremely reserved.

Because of this strict culture, a lot of girls rebel. A traditional Thai girl could never be caught dead casually hooking up with a western guy. If you met her outside of Thailand she would be fair game, but within Thailand people judge and there are strict social rules. So girls rebel, and once they do, they might as well just go all the way and become a bar girl. Prostitution in Thailand is very different from anywhere else in the world. It's almost not looked down upon any more than having a manual labor job such as construction for men.

A big majority of bar girls are from small villages in the north east of Thailand know as Isan which you'll often see misspelled as Isaan, Isarn, Issan, Essan or Esarn. Isan is the poorest part of Thailand, with a culture influenced by their neighbors in Laos and Cambodia. The only real jobs in Isan are farming and are often hit by drought. So often the boys become Muay Thai fighters and the girls go off to work in bars. Money in exchange for love or sex is seen very differently in Thailand than in most countries. Even if a Thai man falls in love with a Thai girl and wanted to get married, he is expected to pay her family a 40,000 – 300,000 dowery, which is $1,335 - $10,000US.

One reason why I never date Thai girls is because even if she's not a prostitute, it often still feels like she is. The majority of guys I've met that are dating Thai girls think their girl is different, that she's not a bar girl and in fact she's one of the good girls. I never say anything because that would just be rude but 98% of the ones I've met either used to be or still are a bar girl. I've even met quite a few guys, owners of gyms, dive shops, and other expats (an expatriate is a person temporarily or permanently residing in a country and culture other than that of the person's upbringing.) married to Thai women that clearly used to be a bar girl.

I'm sure none of these guys would admit or even like to think about what her wife was doing before they got together, and it's damn sure rude to ask, so it just never gets talked about. But even guys that are just dating a Thai girl normally end up giving her money to send home to her family or something along those lines. They convince themselves that it's just part of the culture and it's perfectly normal, and it is. But personally, I don't like that part of the culture and to me, giving your Thai girlfriend money every month feels exactly the same as paying a prostitute.

However, a lot of guys in America do the same thing with their girlfriends. We just call them sugar daddies, older guys that support their younger hot girlfriend by paying her rent and her credit card bill. To me, that's the same thing as prostitution as well, so it's not just a Thai thing.

Dating Thai Guys: (For female readers)
I've met a lot of White girls that have Thai boyfriends and even husbands. One girl I know, a pretty Canadian girl ended up marrying her tattoo artist, a local Thai guy. They now have a child together and live permanently in Thailand. A lot of girls that come train Muay Thai end up with a Thai boyfriend, especially if they are staying for a few months or longer.

Usually White girls end up dating Muay Thai trainers/fighters, bartenders, or fire dancers. I can see why, they came to Thailand to experience a new culture so why not hook up with a local while you're here. If I ever went to Brazil you can bet I'll want to hook up with a local Brazilian, it's no different for girls.

The majority of the time the girls are the ones that choose the guy. You'll be hit on by a lot of Muay Thai trainers but at the end of the day, it'll most likely be the quite, attractive guy in the corner that you'll have your eye on. My only advice is to see what he's like when he's drunk first, before you commit, as a lot of Thai guys have drinking and jealously problems.

Dating Western/White Girls in Thailand:
It's a bit ironic that I came all the way to Thailand not to date Asian girls. The nice thing about Thailand though is you get girls from all over the world. I've met far more English, European, Australian and Scandinavian girls in Thailand than I ever would have back home in America.

You'll meet girls at your Muay Thai/MMA gym but most of the time it won't be anything more than friendship. If you do hook up, it'll most likely be the girl that does the choosing. At most gyms there will be 10-20 guys for every 1 girl. Most of these guys are super fit, and are from all over the world. So the girl basically has a choice of who she wants to hook up with, including all the trainers and UFC Fighters that come visit. Most of the time, the girl either feels self conscious about her sweaty body, or she simply doesn't want to hook up with someone at the gym and have everyone see it and talk about it, so most girls that come train usually don't hook up with other guys at the gym.

While working at a Scuba Diving resort, you'll notice that 99% of Western girls are in long term relationships. The reason is because they're away from home and want some stability in their lives. I had a girlfriend the entire time while working in Koh Lanta. We met during the first week we were both there at a dive shop's grand opening BBQ and started hanging out. She was a sweet girl with a charming personality from Finland. There was nothing else to do on the island besides hang out, walk on the beach and take my motorbike to dinner. So that's what we did most nights. We dated for around 7 months and we're still friends until this day. She even came to visit me at Scuba-Junkie in Mabul, with her new boyfriend which was a bit awkward at first but it was really good to see her again.

Lotta and I in Kuala Lumpur on our Visa Run/Holiday

If it wasn't for having a girlfriend, living in Koh Lanta would have been boring. It's a really beautiful island, an ideal honeymoon destination but it was litereally the most boring place I've been to. There was no movie theater, no mall, and only a few restaurants that we would alternate between. It was in Koh Lanta that I developed the stupid idea to fly across the world to Utila in Honduras to do my instructors course. Part of the reason why I have ill feelings towards Utila is because I gave up someone really special to go there. She asked me not to go, and instead to stay in Koh Lanta a while longer then join her on a trip to Bali and to go diving in Mabul. I really liked her, but ended up sticking to my original plan and went to Utila. I don't know if I ever told her this, but I regretted it as soon as I got there. Who knows what would have happened between us if I had stayed.

A year after her, I followed her same journey to Bali and then eventually to Mabul, exactly where we would have went together a year prior. Don't tell her boyfriend this, but the moment I saw her again in Mabul when she came to visit, seeing her smile again, all the feelings that we used to have came gushing right back. For that first minute or two, I wanted to steal her back.

Lotta and I on a trip to George Town, Penang Malaysia.

When I left Koh Lanta, she cried, and said that the reason why it was so sad was because we were breaking up for no reason. We hadn't fought, disagreed even on anything, and we were getting closer and closer each day. I even met her parents when they came to visit and got along with they great.

Meeting Lotta's Parents and Saving her Father's Hand:
Her father, who has been a carpenter for the past 30 years was getting ready to go home and have surgery on both his hands. They were like lobster claws from laying down flooring for so many years. He could hardly open them. The only reason he had put it off this long was because the doctor said he wouldn't be able to work for six months after surgery. He got a second opinion with the same results.

Over dinner, which they kindly paid for, I suggested that he go to my massage therapist, an old Thai Chinese guy that was one of the best in the world I've ever met. I'm a true believe that everyone should get massages at least once a month, if not every week. It's such a good way to relax the body and muscles, especially if you're doing hard training such as Muay Thai or MMA. In the U.S. I could only afford to get a 30 minute massage once or twice a month, but here in Thailand with the average 1 hour massage costing 200 baht ($6.60US) I get at least one or two a week. However, out of the 300 or so massages I've gotten in my life, there has only been around 5 people in the world I ever really fully trusted and felt truly knew what they were doing.

I regretfully forget his name, but the old Chinese thai guy in Koh Lanta was the only person I the world aside from my massage teacher Chuck Fata at University of California, Irvine that I trusted to really go deep and do whatever he felt would benefit me. I had been training Muay Thai and Scuba Diving a lot and after my first fight, I asked him to work on me, whatever it took. For the next hour, people started gathering as they heard a grown man scream in pain. The massage shop is on the beach itself at Funky Fish on Long Beach, and my screams of pain could be heard from a mile away. He pressed so deep into my muscles that I couldn't help but tearing up, it was far worse pain than being kicked, punched and kneed. But by the end of it, I felt incredible. I give him 500 baht instead of the normal 250, but thinking back, I should have given him closer to 1,000. ($33US) as it was well worth every penny.

I recommended Lotta's father to see him, and thought, maybe he could help a little bit, maybe relieve some of the pain. But that following night, something incredible happened. For those who don't know, old Finnish men don't tend to show much expression, especially when sober, but this night he was ecstatic! He ran up to me, waving his right hand, saying look, look, look! Comparing it side by side to his left hand, it was like night and day. The old Thai-Chinese man fixed it. He worked on it for three hours and only had time for one hand that day, but it worked. He went back the next day for the other. I sincerely hope he gave him an amazing tip as surgery and loss of wages for six months would have costed him much more. Three years has now passed since that night and I was curious, so I emailed Lotta asking about her dad's hand and she replied, "He says it's still perfect! But he also said he would never want to go through that again, it was so painful."

Lotta and Johnny present day:
We're still friends, we email and talk once in a while. It was just strange leaving that relationship with no real breakup. But maybe it's better this way, she's back in Finland going to medical school to become a dentist. Who knows if we'll ever see each other again, but I was really happy with the time we had together on Koh Lanta.

Elin the Swedish Girl:
While working at another dive resort, I met a Swedish girl named Elin. Prior to her, I had been hooking up with random tourists and almost on a weekly basis. When you work at a resort, especially on a small island where there's nothing to do but hang out at the bar or go for a walk on the beach afterward, it makes it a good situation to meet and hook up. I was in pretty good shape from just finished a short fight camp at Phuket Top Team and was a bit broken hearted when the first girl I hooked up with. We first hooked up on Christmas, but then she broke it off with me on New Years Eve saying that she felt bad because she had a boyfriend back in England. The only good thing about that short fling was we had managed to have sex everywhere on that island during those six days in between, including at 18m underwater in full scuba gear.

After the Scuba Brit, I ended up randomly sleeping with a really sweet Canadian girl. We were playing a game of monopoly and I invited her back to my room to watch How I Met Your Mother, which was my favorite show back then. Another week had passed and I honestly wasn't even looking for anyone else, but then Elin came along. I saw her on the dock, she was in a bikini and had a full colored tattoo down her ribs which I loved. She reminded me of the girl from the Steig Larsson book that was popular at the time, "The Girl with the Dragon Tattoo." I knew I had to have her, but was super nervous and almost awkward the first time we met. Luckily, as she told me later, she had already decided to sleep with me when she first saw me, before we even spoke. It's funny how guys think we have game and the power, but in reality it's really the girls that do the choosing most of the time.

I still remember the first time we ever kissed. It was after a game of Risk, (yeah I know, I have a thing about board games). We decided to go for a walk on the beach after the bar had closed at midnight. We were alone, the sky dark, the stars were clear and bright. We were holding hands with our toes in the white sand. We kissed, and it was an amazing passionate kiss, and then she did something totally unexpected that made me laugh and fall for her harder at the same time. She pushed me away and called me a slut! For those who have seen the TV show Californication, it reminded me of the episode where Mia randomly punches Hank Moody in the face right when he's about to cum, for no apparent reason.

So there we were, on this beautiful beach kissing passionately. I tried to move her somewhere more private, but she wanted me then and there, in the middle of the beach. We started standing, but ended up with her back in the sand. It was incredible. That continued for the next 6 or 7 days while she was there, we literally had sex everywhere. At one point, the entire resort heard us, and my co-workers wouldn't shut up about it for weeks. We snuck off to a secluded pier, went to other resorts, basically wherever. We were free, and for once, I honestly didn't care what anyone else thought. I could imagine us together, like Bonnie and Clyde taking over the world, doing whatever we pleased without a care in the world what anyone else thought of us. It was truly the best sex of my life, it was so free and passionate, uninhibited, raw and immersive. After all of the random encounters with girls in my life, I finally met someone that I connected with deeply and passionately on another level.

After Elin left, I was still infatuated, for the rest of the six months I was there I didn't have the desire to hook up with anyone else and slept with no one new. The Norwegian's have a word for it, Forelsket, that doesn't easily translate into English but basically means the euphoria you feel when you are first falling in love.

Every day, new beautiful girls would arrive on the island, but I never hooked up with any of them. The Canadian girl that I had met her a week before Elin came was an exception She came to visit me for a second time. I didn't want to have any regrets, as I had no idea if I was ever going to see Elin again, so we hooked up and had an amazing couple days together. That too passed, and instead of hanging out in the bar, I would be on Skype with Elin figuring out how we could see each other again. She wanted me to meet her in Australia and I thought about it, but I had promised one of my closest friends that I wouldn't. But I remember my good buddy Nic specifically saying to me once.

"Johnny Bro, promise me one thing, promise me that you'll never move to Australia for some chick."

When he had told me that, it had nothing to do with Elin, I hadn't even met the girl with the Dragon Tattoo then. But Nic had given up everything and moved from London to Sydney to be with his girlfriend, and it had all gone bad. He went into debt, lost all of his jiu-jitsu clients and was lonely and depressed in Australia. Learning from his mistakes, I had a bad feeling and knew that I shouldn't meet Elin in Oz.

I convinced her to instead, meet me in the U.S. We planned a cross-country road trip together where we were going to start in California and drive across all the way to Florida and back. 4,467.6 km each way, not including all the detours and stops we had planned to make. For months we planned this trip, and finally, in June of 2012 we saw each other again, this time at LAX, the Los Angeles International Airport. There I was, holding a sign, a teddy bear and a smile on my face when she jumped up into my arms and gave me a kiss.

I don't know when exactly, but then it all started going down hill. She was different, maybe I was different. She blamed it on being in the city, saying that everything is different when you're on a romantic tropical island. But I refuse to believe that. Till this day, I remember what she was like, what we were like together, carefree, and adventurous. It turns out that Elin wasn't the one for me. The sex went from immersive and incredible to exactly the opposite. I could tell there were things on her mind and instead of it being a carefree experience it became over thought. I know some of you may be thinking that sex shouldn't be everything in a relationship, and it's not, but I truly think that with the right person, it could be blissful like what we had on Mabul island in the middle of Borneo. It could be, and should be perfect. Instead, we were driving down the coast of California together, barely speaking only 7 days into the trip. I had one final stop to make before we started driving east, it was an adventure race that I had been training for all year, the Tough Mudder.

Surviving the Tough Mudder:

I had done the same race exactly one year prior, up in Lake Tahoe in Northern California. I thought I had prepared for it, I was in good shape, running a few times a week, being able to pump out 20 pullups in a row. But then it hit me. 13.1 miles/21km of trails straight up and down a mountain was no joke. It was the same distance of a half marathon but instead of being flat land, it was up mountain normally used for skiing. There were also 24 obstacles designed by the British Special Forces, ranging from walls to climb, tunnels to crawl through, ice cold lakes to swim across and ropes to climb.

I quickly realized what I had signed up for and told my teammates, the NorCal Ninjas, to go ahead without me. I was determined to finish, but I knew I had to do it at my own pace. I kept pushing forward, using other familiar faces to keep on track. There was a group all in red t-shirts with their family names printed on their back. They seemed to be going at the same pace as me and they basically adopted me into their group. I was pretty good at all of the obstacles, as I stupidly spent most of my time training pullups and not hiking mountains. One obstacle I really wanted to be able to complete without falling into the water were the monkey bars. As we hiked, ran and crawled our way though the obstacles, it seemed like every time I started losing hope, I'd see a girl that I recognized. She was the girl with a turtle shell backpack and the slogan,

"Slow but steady wins the race."

She became both my motivation and my pace keeper even though we had never spoken, only exchanged smiles.

As the last two miles approached, I was completely gassed and my tank was empty. I told my newly adopted family to go on without me, and to look for me at the beer tent. They offered to stay, an entire team that I had just met that day, felt compassionate enough to stay with me, but I sent them on their way and told them I'd meet them at the finish line. I was completely out of it by the time the finish line neared. My original plan was to finish the race in good time, do the 18 pullups required to win an Army T-Shirt, and enjoy a few beers. Instead, I found myself crawling to the finish line where I forced down a free Myoplex protein shake, tried to enjoy my free Dos Esquis beer, and ended up sucking down bottles of water and wandering around like a zombie trying to go home and die. I had completed my first tough mudder with my good friends Hanley Chan, Nat and his friend Ryan. It was a humbling experience that I thought I would never ever do again. But that week, with Elin, we were driving to Running Springs, CA from San Diego so I could do it all over again for a second time, this time with my cousin Jacob.

Tough Mudder NorCal 2011

Elin and I spent one last night together in a small motel room near where I would be competing the next day. When she kissed me in the morning and wished me good luck, I had no idea that would also be our farewell. We had been fighting all week and we both knew being stuck in a car together for the next 6 weeks would be a nightmare. She cut her trip short and went back to Sweden. I guess Nic was right, and I have to thank him for his advice, or else I would have been the one flying home early from Australia instead of already being home in the U.S.

My friend Nat and cousin Jacob showed up bright and early at the motel that next morning after trying to scare me by calling from the parking lot saying that they had just woken up and were still two hours away. I said good bye to Elin, and we prepared for the battle in front of us. To my surprise, the second time around was much easier. I definitely trained harder for this one and was in much better shape, but it was also shorter at only ten miles instead of twelve. In preparation I had been hiking a lot the past few months, ending it in a massive climb up the highest peak in South East Asia, Mt. Kinabalu in Borneo. From Thailand, it's a manageable flight to jump from Bangkok to Kota Kinabalu through Singapore. The reason why I include Borneo in this book about Thailand is because to me, it's all South East Asia and once you're here, you might as well explore a bit further. Borneo was truly an amazing place. Climbing Mt. Kinabalu was by far the most difficult thing I've ever done in my life. I remember once, seeing a poster at Phuket Top Team saying:

"For once in your life, train with the will to die."

I never really knew that that meant until the second day of the climb up to 4,095m/13,435 ft. I thought I knew how to push myself, I had been in four muay thai fights by then, and had trained to exhaustion countless times. But seeing the peak of the mountain, the summit that I had promised myself I'd reach no matter what, in the distance was my new hell. We were racing to make it to the summit by sunrise, which is why we left at 3am to start. The day's trek started in pitch black, with nothing more than our headlamps to light our way, and as we slowly hikes towards the peak, I could see the sun start to peek over the top. I desperately wanted to just push through the last kilometer or so, but I literally had nothing left. My muscles had given out long ago and were demanding more oxygen than the high altitude would give, and my lungs felt like they were shriveled down to the size of a pea.

I decided then and there that making it to the top was worth dying for, which was a thought that had never previously occurred to me about anything. Statistically, very few people have died on Mt. Kinabalu compared to Mt. Everest, but at that moment, in the freezing cold morning, walking on slippery granite pulling myself up on a top rope, I sincerely felt that there was a chance my heart would give out at any moment and I was okay with it. I thought about my life, what I've accomplished, places I've been and I figured that I had done more than the average person would in 70 years. I was at peace with what ever may have happened. It was then I stopped looking up at the summit. My only goal was to take three steps at a time, allowing myself to rest and catch my breath at each interval. I had gone through the rest of my Snickers chocolate bars which I had been using for quick energy, and the only thing left was heart and desire. This experience has truly made me a better person, and improved my training in Muay Thai and MMA now knowing how much further we can physically push ourselves than we imagine.

I didn't allow myself to look up to the finish anymore, so instead, during my rest breaks, I would look back and where I had just come from. It was surprising, even three steps at a time, was enough to make it a generous distance that I had previously though impossible. Also seeing the people behind me struggling just as much gave me comfort knowing I wasn't the only one. I once heard a quote along the lines of,

"Compare yourself with people who have less than you, rather than those who have more."

There will always be people more fit, naturally athletic, younger, stronger, and it's good to aim to better yourself, but at the same time, we often forget about all of the people that struggle just as hard as we do. With perseverance, I somehow made it to the top of the world.

Hiking in Thailand:
The highest point in Thailand is Doi Inthanon, near Chiang Mai which is 2,565 meters (8415 feet) high. It's also the coldest place in Thailand and the only place it snows, as temperatures can get down to zero degrees. Unfortunately it is a tourist attraction with no hiking trails, only a road that drops you off 10 minutes from the top.

Chiang Mai and nearby Pai however, both offer really good hikes through the mountains and hill tribe villages. Starting at only 1,500 baht for a 3 day, 2 night hike Chiang Mai offers possibly the cheapest trekking package in the world and it includes an elephant ride, white water rafting and all of your meals and accommodation. That's $50US for three days worth of activities, that's crazy cheap! It's also quite fun, but in reality it's more of a tourist backpacker trip than anything, I still recommend it though especially if you happen to get a good group and meet some cool friends.

Koh Tao has a really cool hiking trail that no one ever uses. I used to hike it almost everyday that I had a day off scuba diving in Koh Tao and hardly ever saw anyone else on it. The hike starts just up the hill from Siam Tattoo in Sairee Beach (the main beach), walk up the hill and make a right where the road splits. If you go left, you'll have a very boring unshaded hike to a place quaintly named Mango Bay. Going right, you'll eventually get to Laem Thain bay where you'll find an abandoned resort, still with great cliff diving and snorkeling. Legend has it that the Laem Thian Resort's owner Ping Pong was a bit crazy and one day packed a bag in haste and left to avoid unpaid debts. The road going to Laem Thian got destroyed during the monsoon rains, leaving fissures impassable by bike or car, so the only way was by long tail boat around the island. The bills started piling up and made the resort more expensive to keep open than it was worth. I had thought about camping out there one night and still think it would be a fun idea with a few friends, but it is a bit spooky and might not be the safest thing in the world to do, but if you've read "The Beach" by Alex Garland or seen the movie, this would be an easy place to start a backpacker society. Also in Koh Tao, if you drive a bit north, there are random trails that you find, I've never seen a single person on any of those, and could never find anyone to go with as everyone thought the best way to spend their holiday was getting drunk and staying up late every night, becoming too hungover to do anything active. As for other parts of Thailand, aside from Phuket where I couldn't reasonably find anywhere to hike, there is always something. Thai people in general never hike for pleasure as it involves the sun and exercise, two things that they try to avoid, but the good news is within a short flight from Bangkok, you'll find some of the best hiking trails and mountains in the world to conquer.

Getting Paid to Live and Work on Tropical Islands:
Before coming to Thailand I used to day dream about living on a lush tropical island in the middle of no where. When the TV show "Lost" first aired, I was working in a cubical for a large American corporation, and the highlight of my week was talking about that week's latest episode to my coworkers. I had actually wished I could trade places and be in a plane crash somewhere on a tropical island. Ten years later, having lived and worked on some of the most beautiful islands in the world, I took it so much for granted that I actually left it out of the first version of this book, forgetting how amazing it is to most people. The first island I lived on was Koh Tao, the same story happens to everyone. When they first arrive, they love it, exploring the beaches, secluded bays, snorkeling all day and having drinks on the beach to a beautiful sunset. Then one day, usually after around six months, they hate it and can't wait to leave. But the saying is, "you'll be back." And it's almost always true. Personally I never thought I'd go back but I did, and I'm almost considering doing it again. It's just such an easy place to live.

Koh Lanta the second island I lived on, was beautiful as well. When I first arrived in November the main beach called long beach, was empty. It was a mile of white sand beach and I was the only person on it in the middle of the day. After Christmas when it became busier, long beach would start filling up, but there were 26 more miles (41km) worth of pristine beaches to explore. Unfortunately due to erosion from building up the beach front properties there wasn't any coral left for snorkeling or diving off of the shore. This forced dive companies to buy bigger, more luxurious boats and take trips further out. As a customer you would have to pay around 5,000 baht ($160US) for a day trip but it was absolutely worth it if you were on your honeymoon or just there for a few weeks. There were really only a few different trips but they were all magical with their own charms.

First there was Koh Haa, the five islands. In the middle of the islands was a clear, unspoiled blue water lagoon. The snorkeling and diving around the islands were amazing, some of the best in Thailand and underwater you could see up to 30-40 meters in visibility. Once I even got vertigo, from the water being so clear you couldn't take it all in at once and lost your orientation. It was at Koh Haa that I scuba dove with my only Manta Ray and first ever Whale Shark. Also at Koh Haa there was a beautiful underwater Cathedral, an underwater cave that you could pop up in, take off your regulator and mask and look around with an emerald light glowing from the water.

Then there was Koh Rok, which was somewhat boring diving but had a cave that was unbelievable. The island is surrounded by rock at all sides and the only way in is by snorkeling through the emerald cave, after around 10 minutes of darkness, you start to see a light which opens up to a hidden white sand beach. The first time I swam into it, I instantly thought how amazing it would be to get married there.

But the most remote island I've liven on by far was Mabul island in Borneo. It's a tiny island with just a few resorts and a local fishing village. The company I worked for was an all inclusive resort which meant no one had to carry any cash on them, ever. Breakfast, lunch and dinner were all free to the guests and staff, and everyone had a bar tab. The staff were giving a per diem, a bar allowance good for around three or four beers a night. I never used mine up as I'm not a big drinker, and every time I would go to the bar one of the guests I had taken out diving would insist on buying me a round so I often cashed out the balance at the end of the month.

The first two months on that island were incredible, it was almost the same as being on the best vacation of my life, only I was actually being paid for it. Every morning we would go on day trips to different parts of the island or to other near by. Below is a photo I took of a good friend and co-worker of mine during one of our day trips. It's one of those things that while I was doing it, I loved it. But unfortunately, island fever is real. Thinking back, it sounds stupid, selfish and unappreciative of me, but as amazing was it was after a few months you really want off the island and can't think of anything but ways to complain. I'm glad I finally fulfilled my dream of living on a beautiful remote island, but maybe you're better off just going there as a tourist or for no more than 12 weeks at a time. A dream job is at the end of the day, still a job and as humans we can get tired of anywhere, no matter how gorgeous.

Back to Koh Phangan and the Full Moon Party:

Possibly the greatest party on Earth according to Maxim Magazine, "the ultimate men's magazine." The Full Moon Party on the island of Koh Phangan, Thailand is the only place on Earth you can go out get laid, go to sleep, just to wake up a few hours later and get laid again.

When I had first read the article five years before I ever set foot in Thailand, I thought to myself, wow, really? I had tried figuring out what the island would look like, where to sleep, and in my mind it was a tiny island with no hotels on it, just a lush tropical deserted island with no facilities. Turns out, I was a bit wrong on what the island itself looks like, but one thing holds true, it's quite possibility the best place on Earth to have a one night stand.

I mentioned a bit before that the first time I went to the full moon party I hooked up with an English girl and then ended up with a Thai girlfriend for the rest of the week. Well, I didn't learn my lesson and ended up going back quite a few more times. To me, the FMP is an escape from my daily live of training Muay Thai and MMA or even Scuba Diving when I was working in that field. While everyone else on Koh Tao, went out every night until 2 in the morning, I was in bed by 10. I hardly ever hooked up on Koh Tao, even though it was an island full of young backpacker tourists. The couple times I did, it was the same story as everyone else. I went out to a bar to pre-party, moved down to the beach to watch the thai guys spinning fire, while also moving on to harder liquor fueled by red bull and thai whiskey. We'd party until 3 or 4 in the morning, sometimes even staying up to watch the sunrise, and then in a drunken state, I'd pull a girl back to my room and hook up. Then the next day, I'd feel like shit and have to go to work.

So instead of doing that on a daily basis, which quite a few people I know did, I saved it all up to go all out once a month or once every two months at the full moon party. To be honest, I don't remember all the girls I hooked up with but I do remember that most of the time it wasn't on the full moon night itself, but instead on the nights leading up to the big party. The problem with the FMP is you get so wasted every night you are there, that the nights end up blurring together and by the end of it you remember next to nothing. Girls love the experience just as much as guys do, it's truly a freeing experience to live a hedonistic lifestyle even for one night.

I specifically remember one girl I hooked up with, she was the first Russian girl I had ever been with. She had a really pretty face and a fantastic body, but hardly spoke any English. We met somehow on the beach while dancing, it was my first night on the island, which was 3 nights before the actual full moon party. She was wearing a dress and dancing seductively with me on the sand near the water, we started kissing under the moon light and our hands started to wander. Suddenly I found my hands between her thighs, and felt the warmth of her. I was hesitant at first, but I could sense that she didn't want me to stop, so I allowed my fingers inside of her. Everything else was a blur, we were both lost in the moment and didn't even notice the thousands of other people dancing around us. I ended up taking her hand and leading her towards a hotel that I had stayed it previously, knowing there were secluded spots not to be seen. We ended up on someone's first floor balcony away from the crowds and the music, I took off her panties and entered her. It sounds romantic I know, two strangers from opposite sides of the world, only able to communicate through our emotions and sex, making love in a public place just 100 meters away from the party. But it wasn't romantic at all, it was exciting sure, but I was also dehydrated beyond belief and more drunk than I would like to admit. I ended up stopping half way through and telling her I desperately needed water. At that point I felt more dehydrated than I ever had in my life, having sex with her was like running a marathon through arid desert heat and I felt like I was going to collapse at any point.

I tried to hand her back her panties, a lacey black thong that I still remember, but she gave me a wicked smile and told me to leave it. A little surprise to whoever was staying there that night. We went back to the party, got me a bottle of water and danced for a bit before deciding to leave. I started walking her back to her bungalow which was quite a far walk away from the beach, rehydrated yet incomplete, I ended up pulling her into the back of a coffee shop that was open air and unlocked. We laid on the ground on a cushion and continued our little session until we were both completely satisfied. I walked her the rest of the way up the hill to her room where I kissed her goodbye as she walked up the stairs to her room. My last memory of my little Russian doll was her smiling and lifting up her skirt to remind me she still wasn't wearing any panties as she snuck back into her room.

That night I was exhausted and completely happy, but the very next day, I felt a void. The problem with drunken one night stands Is that it's really not that satisfying. You have flash backs of images and memories but that's really about it. Over the course of the next few days, I was hoping to bump into her again but with thousands of people arriving on the island everyday it wasn't likely. I even tried to retrace my steps to look for where I had dropped her off at, but for the life of me, I couldn't find the room again. Maybe it was for the best, or maybe if I hadn't been so drunk, I would have made a plan with her for the next day. Who knows what she would have wanted, maybe in her mind, she was happy with the random one night stand with the guy she met on the beach.

Aside from the Russian beauty, there were others, but to be honest, I honestly can't recall much about them. Most of the time, it didn't lead to sex however, it was just kissing and making out. I remember one night I had met a German girl, a really stunningly beautiful girl that was in Thailand working on a project for her masters degree. We met early in the night before we both started drinking, and hung out for hours after. I don't know why, but I couldn't figure her out. I never made a move on her as I had no idea if the other guy she was traveling with was just her coworker or a love interest. But I was definitely attracted to her, but then, the craziest thing happened. Another German girl, who looked like she could be her twin, came along and started chatting with us. They both looked at each other and before leaving, the twin kisses me good bye. But it wasn't just a peck, it was a full on romantic kiss on the lips that felt like it lasted a few minutes, all while the girl I was with stood right beside us. It had felt like I had finally kissed the girl I had been attracted to all night, but at the same time, it wasn't her, it was like kissing a clone.

Stranger things have happened, especially when it comes to kissing during the craziness of the full moon party. I still remember the first Swedish girl I ever kissed, I wasn't that drunk yet at that time and vividly remember how beautiful she was. She was a natural platinum blonde with highlights from the sun, in her early twenties with striking blue eyes, but clearly she wasn't the best listener in the world. She approached me with her friend and a random Thai guy and asked me if I was Thai. I told her that I was American but I've been living in Thailand for a while now. And the Swedish beauty responded,

"I've always wanted to kiss a Thai guy."

Turns out that Thai guy that was with her friend was their tattoo artist and she too wanted an authentic Thai guy of her own. I quite obviously wasn't it, but I guess in her mind she had her mind made up that I was close enough. She then kissed me, and it was amazing. It was like kissing a mythical unicorn for the first time. She was beautiful, flawless even and she wouldn't be the last girl that would kiss me thinking I was Thai.

Chiang Mai – My Favorite city in Thailand

If I was going to pick one city in Thailand that would be the best for hooking up with normal western girls, it would be Chiang Mai. The absolute worst places to hook up with White girls are Phuket, Pattaya and Bangkok.

In Phuket and Pattaya, even though there are plenty of normal girls that go there, they are so disgusted by the sex tourism that the last thing they want to do is feel like a whore. In Bangkok, you have some of the same but also with the added danger factor. If you're going to get ripped off or scammed, it'll most likely happen in Bangkok, as it's the first stop for unsuspecting tourists. Everyone's guard is up and it's not an ideal place for romance.

Chiang Mai however, is peaceful, stress free and safe. By the time you get to Chiang Mai, you are already pretty comfortable with the do's and don'ts in Thailand and can let your guard down. No one comes to Chiang Mai for sex tourism so everyone you meet traveling are relatively normal and mostly young with good intentions. Every time I've been in Chiang Mai I've met a really cool girl that I ended up sight seeing with and really enjoying my time with. The only other place in the world that made me feel the same was Antigua, the old capital of Guatemala. Maybe it's because both cities have history and are both a large square town surrounded by walls, or maybe it's the abundance of artists, students and English teachers that make up the crowd. Either way, it's my favorite place to hook up with a normal girl, and not just for a one night stand. Out of everywhere in Thailand, Chiang Mai is possibly the only place I could ever see myself really living long term, even retiring in. It's also the only place I could see myself having a normal relationship and a normal life. There are still a few places to party, but it's really not a party town. You have the local Thai places that are authentic and fun, and you have my favorite place of all, the square containing Zoe in Yellow and Roots, Rock, Reggae. It was there, during the night of the Songkran water festival that it happened to me again. This time I was completely smashed from drinking a flask of Hong Thong Thai Whiskey combined with some Xanax. It was my first, and last time ever doing Xanax and it was given to me by some girl at my hostel. She had warned me that mixing it with alcohol might make me black out, but at the time it sounded like a good idea.

I was so messed up I could hardly speak, causing an American girl I met that night to think I was actually Thai. Just like the Swedish girl I had met on the beach in Koh Phangan I guess this girl was looking forward to hooking up with a local guy as well, and it turns out it was going to be me that night. We kissed a bit outside of the nightclub Zoe in Yellow and I ended up taking her hand and leading her back to my hostel. It was a 10 minute walk away, and half way through she asked me where we were going. In my slurred English, I mumbled something about "just there" and pointed. My roommate at the hostel, this Dutch girl named Leonie was still at the party so we had the room to ourselves, I don't remember much about the sex aside that she had a beautiful full body tattoo. I was a bit mad at Leonie for leading me on the past two weeks and springing the "let's just be friends talk" on me that day before. So the very next night, I did the exact same thing again, this time with a Canadian girl that I remember almost nothing about.

This time however, Leonie was in the room sleeping. To be fair, I had told the Canadian girl that someone was sleeping inside and that we should go somewhere else, but she insisted. I tried getting her to go into the bathroom with me, but she pushed me down on the bed, which was the lower bunk and got on top of me. One minute later, I hear Leonie climb down the ladder, utterly pissed off at what just happened. We had woken her up both with the Canadian girl's moans but also rocking the flimsy metal bunk bed. I honestly don't know if I did it out of spite but twenty minutes later after we were done, I found Leonie furiously angry sitting in the hallway waiting for us to have finished.

The next day, after two weeks of traveling and sharing a room together, Leonie and I parted ways. I couldn't tell if she was angry, disappointed or otherwise upset with me, but when she said goodbye, I could sense it wasn't just anger. Maybe she did have some feelings for me and was hurt when I took another girl home. But either way, she was the one to declare us just friends so what the fuck did she want me to do about it?

The French Girl in Chiang Mai:
As I'm writing this, it was New Years Eve two nights ago and I decided to go into town to celebrate. I'm currently training at KC Muay Thai which is 25 minutes away in the countryside of Chiang Mai. This was also the first New Years Eve since I turned 16 that I didn't drink, do drugs or otherwise get fucked up. I stayed at a little hostel where I met a ton of cool people traveling around the world and ended up going to dinner with a group. It was Mexican food, and although the free chips and salsa were quite good, the actual food itself wasn't, especially compared to what we have in California.

After dinner we stopped by 7-Eleven to get drinks to pre-party back at the hostel. I didn't really have a reason not to drink, but three months ago, I had decided to stop and focus on my health and training. That morning I had been mentally deciding whether or not to break my 3 month sober streak but ended up deciding nothing more than:

"let's just see what happens."

A little bit before midnight we went back to Thaepae Gate, where the main countdown was to be held. We lit paper lanterns for good luck and made a wish. Here I am making a wish for the new year before releasing the lantern into the sky. Nothing happened that night aside from a bit of fun dancing and having fun. I stayed sober aside from a few red bulls and sodas even when I was offered free drinks by three different girls that night. It was a bit of a difficult situation but ended up keeping level headed and focused on my health and fitness instead.

People say that every time you go out drinking, you lose an entire week's worth of cardio and fitness that you had worked so hard for, and I believe them. My goal for this year has been to dedicate myself to Muay Thai and getting in the best shape of my life, whatever it takes. So even though I'm quite sure I could have hooked up with someone that night if I had loosened up a bit and had some drinks, it wasn't my priority.

The next morning however, I ended up bumping into the French girl that I had been hanging out with the night before. She had left the group early without saying bye, as she wanted to sneak away to bed before it got too late. I was on my way to explore a part of the city and go to a park that I had never seen before and invited her along with me. It was really nice, I got to see a part of Chiang Mai that I assumed I had been to but in reality it was my first time. Before getting to the park we stopped by an archery range that is now on my to do list, had some lunch at a local thai restaurant and even thought about buying a baby hedgehog at a pet store. We also stopped by a few temples and even a free museum along the way. Eventually we got to the park, rented a bamboo mat for 10 baht (33cents) and laid out together in the sun for the rest of the afternoon. It was nice, and it was a change of pace for me. For the last two months my focus was strictly to eat, sleep and train, and I was surrounded by testosterone. Everyone I hung out with at the gym was a guy, and even the few women at the gym were focused on their masculine energy. So to lay around in a park, with a girl in my arms was refreshing and a good way to rebalance my feminine energy.

We got a few dirty looks for making out in public, a cultural no-no in Thailand and ended up on our way back to the hostel.

I had planned on going home that morning straight after breakfast, but that was before I met Sophie. We bought some clementines, which I refereed to as baby mandarin oranges, and hung out at the hostel until dinner. Turns out for 40 baht, $1.33US you can buy an entire kilo worth of them and it's much more than any two people can eat, so we shared it with the rest of the hostel and still had some left over. For dinner, we found a random hole in the wall Thai-Chinese restaurant that served the most amazing crispy skinned roast pork and soup I've had anywhere. After dinner we went for a walk along a flower market and river, and ended up back at the moat for another make out session before taking her home. I didn't want to leave but had already checked out of the hostel for the night. I was tempted to get another room somewhere and ask her to stay with me, but I figured I might as well just take her back to my apartment. I was a bit hesitant to ask at first since I live quite far out of the city, so I thought I'd be clever and suggest we go back to my place so she could check out my gym and where I lived.

After we had sex, she laid in my arms, cuddling into the nook of my shoulder. It was then that I knew we could be most honest with each other, so I asked her when she had first become attracted to me, and when she knew she wanted to have sex. I used to think there was something called game, where you could say the right things and seduce any woman you wanted. It turns out that women know what they want long before you cleverly suggest to go back to your place to see your gym. All game really is understanding what women are attracted to, namely being in shape, well groomed, confident, and knowing how to pull the trigger when she gives you hints. In a previous life I wasted years trying to figure out what women wanted and what the perfect conversation should be like. Now that I simply focus on my passions, stay in shape and am confident enough to go after what I want and pull the trigger when she gives me the signal. Now my sex life is better than it ever was, all without having to think about it or play games. I call it designing an attractive lifestyle.

Another good thing about having Sophie over is I finally had the balls to eat at a local thai restaurant near the gym that I had been afraid to go into these past few months. They didn't speak a word of English and had no menus but we somehow figured it out and had a great last meal together before I put her in a taxi on her way. I had planned on training that afternoon but I was exhausted from the long day before and our morning session before she left. The good thing is we both had fun with our little fling, and now I can focus again on what I came here to do, and that is to train.

Another reason why I don't date Thai girls:
One of the reasons why I don't date Thai girls is because they don't leave. It's very normal for a Thai girl to move into your place after you have sex, usually because they share a room with other people and like having a place to themselves. If you have cable TV and air conditioning, expect yourself to also have a live in girlfriend, which is why I'm 100% sure that my best friend from the US would have a girlfriend here in Thailand if he had come, even though he never gets girls back in the states.

It's pretty easy for any western guy to get a Thai girlfriend. You'll often see good looking young western guys with Thai girls, so it's not just a thing old fat German men do. I guess to a white guy, dating an Asian girl is exotic and fun. They like the fact that Thai girls are very submissive, and take care of you. I know it's a bit ironic that I came all the way to Asia to only date White girls, but that's just my personal choice, and as far as Muay Thai is concerned, it's much better for me to have a two day fling with a girl that's traveling than end up with a live in Thai girlfriend that will always be there. Having a girlfriend makes it really easy to be lazy, skip training, spend money and eat unhealthy all of the time.

Just a word of warning, don't settle just because you are comfortable and content. A lot of men, both in Thailand and in America end up marrying a girl that they really aren't passionately in love with, often they don't even have sex after they get married. Marrying a Thai girl to me 99% of the time is the guy falling in love with the idea of settling down with a nice, attractive girl that doesn't bitch at him, argue and treats him like a man. To me, this is settling and being content, almost lazy. Just keep in mind what you're getting yourself into if you make the plunge.

If you asked me four years ago before I really discovered who I was, what qualities my ideal girlfriend/future wife would have, I would have given you a generic list. Honestly, four years ago I would have been happy with any pretty girl that was nice and liked me. Now I know exactly what I want in a girl and in my future wife and who knows if I would have discovered those things if I hadn't traveled. There's a good chance that if I never came to Thailand, I would be married with a kid on the way today, and there's also a good chance I would have settled with a girl that I'd later realize I wasn't passionately in love with because I wouldn't have known any better. My biggest fear used to be waking up one day at 35 or 40 and being single and alone. After seeing how unhappy and unfilled most of my friends are in their marriages my new biggest fear is now waking up married to a women that I fight with all the time, at a job that I hate, and not being able to leave it or her because I have a mortgage and children to think about.

Johnny FD

Chapter 5: Muay Thai and MMA in Thailand

First off, training Muay Thai and MMA here in Thailand is completely different from doing it back home. Mainly because no one here has a full time job or other responsibilities, training basically becomes your job even if you're only here for 2 weeks. A lot of pro fighters move from Vancouver Canada to Montreal to train at Tristar where GSP and other pro fighters train, mainly because in Vancouver, people have jobs. At tristar training is their job.
I've trained at some decent gyms in San Francisco and San Diego, California but it's always been the same story, people work and are tired from work so they try to keep the classes as short as possible. Most classes outside of Thailand are 1 hour. You also have insurance problems and lawsuits making gyms hesitant to let you spar hard, or spar at all sometimes. Having a fight after only 2 or 3 months of training would be completely out of the question in America or anywhere else in the world, but in Thailand, it's perfectly normal and almost expected.

My warms up here in Thailand are basically the same as an entire workout back home. Going for a 2.5 mile (4km) run back home is a once a week achievement but here it's a warm up run before every workout. Lifting weights at the gym is a workout back home, but here it's what we do on our rest days. Saturday sparring sessions is a once a week event as well, but three to five rounds of sparring is standard in every class here, every single day. So make sure you come in shape because you'll need it.

Most Muay Thai gyms offer training twice a day, 6 days a week with Sunday being the standard rest day across the country. MMA gyms have the same schedule but with grappling classes sprinkled in as well.

Typical day's schedule here at KC Muay Thai in Chiang Mai.
Most other gyms I've trained at follow a similar schedule.

Warm Up Run: 2.3miles (3.7km)
Jump Rope Skipping: 3-15 minutes (depending)
Shadow Boxing: (2 rounds)
10 Pushups and Situps between every round (90 total of each)
Pad work/Bag work: Usually you do 3 rounds of each. Some days you do up to 5 rounds of pad work

Sparring/Clinching: Everyday rotates between Muay Thai Sparring, Boxing Only Sparring and Clinching. 3 to 5 rounds.

Technique/Conditioning: Most days we do 200-300 knees and/or push kicks or we do 100 kicks with partners on the bag, or practice some type of technique with partners.

Group situps: Everyone in a circle leads an exercise, either situps, bicycles, or pushups, and counts to 20.

Group Stretching: Really nice to all stretch together as we all know it's important, we're just usually too lazy to do it on our own.

Optional Strength Conditioning: For those with a bit of energy left, you can do pullups, kettle bells or weights.

How to get in shape before coming to Thailand:
The majority of people show up and need 2-4 weeks just to get in shape to survive the class. Do yourself a favor and come in with great cardio. My first trip I made the mistake of lifting weights at home thinking that would somehow make me in good enough shape for Muay Thai, I was wrong. This time I biked a lot and ran a bit before coming, thinking my cardio was decently good. I was wrong again.

Three things that will really hurt your cardio in the beginning is jet lag, the heat, and small Thai portions of food that you won't be used to. So if you want to be able to run 2.3 miles in the Thai sun, make sure you can run 4 miles back home. Immediately follow your runs with 100 burpees with pushups. You can divide them up in 5 sets of 20, just make sure you get through 100 with good form. If you can do that, you'll be in pretty good shape to start training right away. You also do the burpee pyramid which I'm a fan of. You start with 10, shadowbox for 10-30 seconds, do 9, shadow box, 8, then 7, 6 and so on. Once you get down to the last one, you've done a total of 55. If you still have energy, repeat it for a second round. You may also want to start jumping rope back home as we do it here in Thailand before every training, if for no other reason than to get your technique down and some base jump rope cardio going, shoot for three five minute rounds of jump rope.

If you can do the run and the burpees twice a day six days a week back home, you'll be able to train twice a day here in Thailand. But if you can't, you might want to have more realistic training expectations. For me personally, I am happy training just once a day, 5 days a week, taking Sundays and either Wednesday or Thursdays off depending on how I feel. I also alternate between a long runs and shorter warm up jogs every other day just to change things up a bit. Also take it easy the first couple weeks when you're here, I see it all the time. Guys show up, give it their all twice a day, then get sick or injured and don't train the rest of their trip.

To be honest, even if you did the most lax training schedule ever and only trained Monday, Wednesdays and Fridays, taking four days off a week you'd still be in amazing shape if you did it for 6 months straight. You'd actually be a much better fighter and and in better shape than the guy that trains twice a day six days a week but is only here for a month. There really is no substitution for time.

Where to Train: Best Gyms in Thailand
I get this question asked a lot on my blog. "Bro, I want to come to Thailand and train, where should I go?"

Here's the official answer, and it's a bit different for everyone.

The biggest factor is where in Thailand to train, finding a gym itself is quite easy. Most guys go to Phuket for their first trip as it has everything. The weather is good all year, there are nice beaches, it's close to nice islands, and it's very foreigner friendly, you won't need to speak a word of Thai. There are a ton of both Muay Thai and MMA gyms to chose from and lots of information on how to book a few weeks or longer there.

Tiger Muay Thai in Phuket was my first real "fight camp" experience. I had trained at Lanta Muay Thai in Koh Lanta but it was more of just a gym and not an experience. At TMT you could live, eat, sleep, and train at the gym, making you feel just like a contestant on The Ultimate Fighter reality series. It was there I met my first UFC Fighters, Roger Huerta and Royce Gracie. I also met one of my current best friends, Nicolas Gregoriades who was a guest Brazilian jiu-jitsu coach and also happens to be Roger Gracie's first black belt. While writing this paragraph, Nic just messaged me on facebook, maybe he felt me talking about him:

"Bro, I'm very seriously considering spending at least 3 months there towards the end of the year or early next year You are so, so right. My rent alone here is 1200 dollars a month...

I want to write my book but I literally don't have time because I'm always on a train to work, or working or exhausted from work

600USD per month budget is amazing - I'm saving up so I can just come out there and not have to work. Just hang with you and run my online businesses etc.
I had a major epiphany the other day - I realized that my life is and has always been about the quest for 'ultimate freedom'"

It's been 4 years since we both first met at Tiger Muay Thai, he was teaching a seminar, I stuck around to tell him that he looked like Tim Ferris, my favorite author. Turns out we had a ton in common and become really good friends after that. We traveled to Koh Phi Phi for a weekend vacation, and when it was time to say good bye, we said instead, "I'll see you later."

We did, we hung out again in San Francisco, and a year later in San Diego, and hopefully, very soon this year he'll pack up his shit in London and move to Chiang Mai.

So if you want to live the "Ultimate Fighter" reality show and meet people you've seen on TV, then Tiger Muay Thai is the gym that brings the most to Thailand. Phuket Top Team just down the street also has a lot of fighters visiting, mostly from more Asian and Australian based shows. I met and hung out a lot with Will "the kill" Chope while at PTT, as you may recall from the living in a rat dwelling experiment I had. Either way, Phuket is fun and a good choice to go to, especially if it's your first time in Thailand.

The Best Gym in Phuket:
One of the most common questions I get on my blog is what gym is better, Tiger Muay Thai or Phuket Top Team. I never answered the question directly, for a few reasons. One is I trained at both and left both gyms on good terms, so I

never wanted to piss anyone off by siding with one gym or the other. But secondly, I honestly enjoyed my time at both gyms virtually equally. It was a perfect situation for me, I first went to Tiger Muay Thai because they had a really clear website and offered on site accommodation which was a non-negotiable must have for me. My first trip was only for 7 days, but I loved it so much I went back again for 3 months. The sheer size, popularity and good business management of TMT also led to some of it's downsides. Mainly, the classes are really large especially the beginner and intermediate Muay Thai Classes. The beginners class has too many students for the instructors to hold pads for, so it becomes more of a carido based class. I wouldn't go as far as saying it's carido kickboxing, as it's still Muay Thai technique based, but it's a lot of bag work, and carido.

The intermediate class at TMT was pretty good, you got to do pad work daily and spar once in a while. However, it seemed like we had to clinch way too often verses sparring. My main gripe with the intermediate class was that the schedule was set in stone and would simply repeat itself, making the class become very mundane. I guess it was a good thing because it encouraged me to move up to Advanced which was the best class of all. Smaller groups and varied training, every day was a different structured class and we did things like king of the ring sparring which was really tough but also fun and a great workout. Another random drill we did was only defend for three minutes then switch. It was on that day I really got comfortable being hit and keeping my eyes open. TMT was able to do these type trainings since everyone in the class is on the same level. I don't think it would have worked as well for a mixed class. I never trained in the 4th level, the fighter's only class, but from what I saw it looked very free flowing with more sparring.

One downside if you're only going for a short time like I did on my first trip is TMT makes you either buy all of your own equipment including 16oz gloves and shin guards on sparring days, or you can rent gloves for 200 baht per day. The good thing about it is that everyone uses clean 16oz gloves for sparring, which reduces injuries vs. inconsiderate people at other gyms that will spar you with 12 or 14oz gloves.

Another downside to TMT is they will charge you for everything and a make a commission wherever they can. Renting a motorbike through the office was a lot more expensive than renting one anywhere down the street. Having TMT book you a room at a hotel down the street will cost you 2,000 baht ($66US) a month more than if you did it yourself directly. Everything has a markup on it at TMT, but it's also a good service for people coming to Thailand for the first time and need their hand held. If you're only coming for 2 weeks and don't mind paying a little extra, TMT's office has English speaking staff that will happily arrange everything for you. You will get an overall good training experience in both Muay Thai and MMA, plus they have nice little extra classes such as Yoga, or once a week Muay Thai on the beach. If you can get a room on the camp itself, it's a really nice experience even though the rooms are a bit old and you need to share a bathroom.

Then comes Phuket Top Team, basically PTT took everything good about Tiger Muay Thai and made it more intimate. The PTT camp is 1/3 of the size of the

TMT campus, and is built to accommodate a lot less people. Tiger Muay Thai can host around 300 students during high season, and Boyd, PTT's owner said he was going to cap attendance at 50, whether he does it or not I have no idea, but that was the original plan.

The reason why I chose to train at Phuket Top Team instead of Tiger Muay Thai on my subsequent training camp was because PTT was brand new, sponsored by Fairtex with all new gear, and I really liked the idea of a smaller, dark horse type gym with the motto, "No Egos, Only Dedication." What I liked about PTT was the classes were a bit shorter, but packed just as much quality into each training, there was less fluff and more pad work, PTT also had the idea to hire only the best trainers from Thailand, and have all of the students be dedicated and training to fight. It was a great idea and I respected it a lot so I joined the gym 2 weeks before it officially opened. I again, lived on the camp itself, the rooms were brand new and very nice. The only problem with the rooms is they could have easily built a window in the back which would have given the rooms a nice cross breeze, but didn't. Also the mattresses were a good size, but really terrible quality making the springs collapse within weeks. I hope they replace them with the harder, thin, thai style mats instead.

The gym was built really quickly, and the design works decently well, but you can tell a lot of things weren't well thought out and could have been better planned if the owner had consulted others or even just simply asked other people for their advice before building it. Little things like, the office door should have faced the gym/main street, instead of being on the side. The L shaped indoor grappling room could have been a wider rectangle instead, and the juice bar should have been in the front or side. But none of that really matters, because over all, the training facility is great, the equipment is top notch, the trainers are good, and the prices are fair.

There are of course, tons of other gyms in the Phuket Area, but PTT and TMT are the only MMA gyms, the rest only focus on Muay Thai. The funny thing is, even though I always trained at MMA gyms, I only did Muay Thai classes 99% of the time. At Tiger I did Yoga once in a while and No-Gi Jiu-Jitsu once a week. At Phuket Top Team I only did Jiu-Jitsu and MMA five times in the 4 months I was there. So I finally asked myself, why don't I just train at a Muay Thai only gym. I looked into Rawai Muay Thai, Dragon, Suwit and Sinbi and visited the gyms to watch one of their training sessions. I thought about training at Suwit since it was a good location, at the end of the street, still relatively near TMT and PTT. Sinbi seemed like a great out of the way gym with nice rooms at the camp itself, but it was ridiculously over priced at 32,000 baht ($1,066US) for 28 days of private room and training, and I've heard the training has gone downhill over the years.

The newest Muay Thai gym in Phuket is Sumalee Boxing Gym also in the Chalong Area, 10 minutes away from Tiger and Phuket Top Team. They have all brand new Twins sponsored gym equipment as of 2012 and have really nice on site accommodation They also have a meal plan which is a good way for people to get fed and hang out at the gym after training. However, their prices are really high as well, almost the same as Sinbi's. Phuket is overall, an expensive place with a money hungry mentality. Everyone from taxi drivers, bar girls, restaurant and gym owners will try to make as much money from you as possible, it's just the way it is in Phuket. Still, if you factor in the cost of food and accommodation, even with the high priced training, living and training in Phuket is still a lot cheaper than it is back home, especially if you come from an expensive country such as Norway, Sweden, or even some parts of the U.K. I would recommend training in Phuket if it's your first time in Thailand and only have a few months or less. It's perfect for a guy in his early 20's that is here for 2, 4, or 8 weeks, especially if you've never been to Thailand before. It's also a very good place to go and for beginners and intermediate MMA.

The two best gyms in Phuket, would definitely be Tiger Muay Thai and Phuket Top Team, even if you are only training Muay Thai. Both gyms have good equipment, are very clean and sanitary, cheap on-site accommodation, and good training. They both on the same street, which has become the Muay Thai and MMA town with tons of restaurants, pharmacies, housing, and massage shops close by. They are a 25-30 minute motorbike ride away from the beaches, and a 15 minute ride away from the Central Mall and Cinema. At both gyms you will meet plenty of other travelers and fighters and you will leave with a good experience.

To answer the burning question everyone keeps asking me, what gym is better, Tiger Muay Thai or Phuket Top Team. I would have to say, overall, Tiger Muay Thai has the slight edge. TMT has more on-site accommodation and much better organized. You also meet a lot more people at Tiger, have opportunities to meet a lot of big named UFC fighters, and bring home some sick ass Tiger Muay Thai T-Shirts. The reason why I give the best gym in Phuket award to Tiger Muay Thai, is even though Phuket Top Team is a very close second, and a better gym in some aspects, TMT is the original and is the reason why every Taxi driver in Phuket knows how to get to the street with the rest of the gyms. TMT put in the effort and money to start up a gym and introduce MMA to Thailand. Ironically, it is because of Phuket Top Team and other competitive gyms that Tiger Muay Thai is still good today. PTT forced TMT to raise the bar, remodel some of their outdated facilities, and build an indoor grappling area. Without PTT and other competition, there was a good chance that TMT would have left the gym get old, raise the prices as they would have been a monopoly and get lazy. Competition is good for everyone.

Phuket Top Team gets the award for best Gi Brazilian Jiu-Jitsu in Thailand and best gym in Phuket for MMA fighters. The owner Boyd has good connections to set you up to fight all around Asia and Australia, and can get you free flights and all expenses paid trips to China to fight MMA. At the end of the day, it's up to you where you want to train. But for me personally, Tiger Muay Thai was the best gym I trained at as a newbie, and I had an amazing time and met some really cool people. Phuket Top Team was an amazing gym for coming back to Phuket for a second fight camp after I had already familiarized myself with Phuket a bit.

The Best Gym in Bangkok:
Bangkok would seem like the logical choice for the best or at least most authentic training in Thailand. There are at least 45 Muay Thai gyms in Bangkok, and also a bunch of Thai only gyms none of us have ever heard of. The two best and most respected stadiums in Thailand, Lumpinee and Rajadamnern Living in Bangkok would also seem like a good idea as they have a sky train, an abundance of metered taxi cabs, great restaurants, nightlife and culture. However, Bangkok is usually the last choice for most people coming to Thailand to train.

Random fact about Bangkok, it's full historical name is actually Krungthepmahanakhon Amonrattanakosin Mahintharayutthaya Mahadilokphop Noppharatratchathaniburirom Udomratchaniwetmahasathan Amonphimanawatansathit Sakkathattiyawitsanukamprasit.
It literally translates to City of angels, great city of immortals, magnificent city of the nine gems, seat of the king, city of royal palaces, home of gods incarnate, erected by Visvakarman at Indra's behest.

Anyways, training in Bangkok is best for people that have to be in Bangkok for another reason such as work or school. I suppose it would also be good for people that love to live in big cities. The best gyms in Bangkok however, are all quite far from the city center. Fairtex Bangplee and Sitmonchai are regarded as the two best Muay Thai gyms in Bangkok but both of them are a far drive away from the city. Fairtex is around 30 minutes away and Sitmonchai is 60-90 minutes away. The problem with Fairtex is because they have a famous name they are also extremely expensive at 18,200 baht ($606US) per week per person for training, a private room with air conditioning and two meals a day. That equates to 72,800 baht a month which is $2,426US. You can share a room with someone else, forgo the aircon and save a bit of money but you'll still end up spending 30,800 baht a month which is $1,026US. Either way, it's over priced and really expensive.

Sitmonchai regarded as the best thai style training out of any gym in Bangkok, and possibly all of Thailand. It's in a small quiet town an hour and a half away from the city, and charges a flat rate of 30,000 baht ($1,000US) a month for training, shared accommodation, 2 meals a day, and they even include motorbike rental, which I've never heard of anywhere else. You can upgrade to having your own private room for 6,000 baht ($200US) more a month or you can find an apartment close by for a lot cheaper, although you may have to furnish it yourself.

Then there's Sitsongpeenong is a little bit cheaper than Fairtex and is around 20 minutes from the city. For the same package including your own room, training, and 2 meals a day for 48,000 baht $1,600US per month which is still a bit on the expensive side. A good friend of my trained at Sitsongpeenong and although it's a very nice looking gym, he didn't recommend it, mainly for the feel and vibe of the gym and trainers.

I've also heard good things about Fighting Spirit Gym which only has shared rooms but is significantly cheaper at 14,000 baht ($466US) a month including training. Fighting Spirit doesn't include food but the food included isn't worth more than 4,500 baht ($150US) a month anyways, still making it significantly cheaper than the top two gyms.

I've trained at 13 Coins in Bangkok, which used to be the gym of the legendary Sanchai Sor Kingstar, but since he's left the gym the training and reputation goes up and down depending on who's there at the time. The 13 Coins gym is actually better known as an airport resort and restaurant that local Thais often frequent. The hotel room I stayed at in 2011 was really nice, brightly lit and the food at the restaurant although expensive was really good. However in recent years the gym is getting old an a bit dated. Training has suffered a bit as well, but they now have an MMA program with a guy named B.K. Brandon Kesler. I would recommend checking out 13 coins if you only have a few days in Bangkok as a layover before a flight. Even though the gym is in the city, there is almost nothing around the area and not that many other people training there so you might get really bored.

The best Muay Thai gym in Bangkok would have to be Sitmonchai although it's quite far outside of the city. Personally I would live and train there and book a hotel in the city every other weekend to get away.
The runner up best gym in Bangkok would be Fighting Spirit Gym mainly for their location within the city center, their low prices, for having MMA/BJJ, and for the fact that they are one of the few gyms that train on Sundays. I've heard that the training itself is decent.

MMA and Brazilian Jiu-Jitsu Gyms in Bangkok:
BJJ and MMA are getting more and more popular around the world and in Thailand. Bangkok has the most BJJ schools of anywhere in Thailand including 3 Monkeeez Jiu Jitsu, Bangkok Brazilian Jiu-Jitsu, Bangkok Fight Club, BJJ Boxer Rebellion, EMAC Thailand, and Fighting Spirit. There are also quite a few BJJ tournaments popping up in Bangkok, mainly through BJJ Asia.

Best Gym in Pattaya:

Personally, I would never train in Pattaya. It's a sleazy town and it really gives Thailand a bad name. I almost guarantee that if you go to Pattaya to train you will end up drinking a lot, hooking up with bar girls, and not dedicating to training. The other guys training at the gym will be doing the same thing, and overall, it won't be a good environment to get fit and train.
The only reason why Pattaya is so popular is because it's relatively close to Bangkok and has a beach, although it's a shitty one. You are better off going down to Phuket if you want to semi-dedicate to training but still want the fun parts of Pattaya.

The best gym in Pattaya is Fairtex but just like the one in Bangplee it is overpriced. The second best gym in Pattaya would most likely be Sityodtong, but honestly bro, I have no idea, Pattaya really isn't my thing. I wouldn't recommend it.

Best Gym in the Koh Tao/Koh Samui/Koh Phangan Area.
There are three islands on the east coast of Thailand that are quite nice places to visit and live. Prices are cheaper than Phuket, which is the west coast, and since the islands are within a 1-2 hour ferry ride from each other, you have some variety. The main draw of Koh Tao is the cheap scuba diving and backpacker lifestyle. Koh Phangan is famous for it's monthly full moon party. Koh Samui is the most built up and expensive of the three islands and is the only one with it's own airport.

The worst gym in Thailand I've ever trained at: Koh Tao.
Koh Tao only has one Muay Thai gym, Island Muay Thai which is up the road next to Monsoon Gym in Sairee Beach. The reason why I was so unhappy with this gym is because it could have been really good and I wish it was. The facilities are okay, and the location is really good. I lived in Koh Tao twice, for six months each time and really wanted a decent Muay Thai gym to train at. The reason why Island Muay Thai is so bad is because the trainers simply don't care. They know they are the only gym on the island, and most of their students are backpackers that don't know anything about Muay Thai so they just smile and take your money without putting in much effort.

The typical class started with jump rope and what seemed like 5 rounds of boring shadow boxing with no instruction. The pad work was terrible, the worst I've had in Thailand. The trainers were lazy and didn't have any heart. I tried a few different trainers including the head trainer, and half the round he would be talking to someone else or otherwise not paying attention. Then they would tell you to do 5 boring rounds on the bags by yourself, with no instruction. That's it. I wondered what the hell I was paying for as I could have done that on my own. We also never sparred or clinched. I'm always surprised when I read positive reviews of Island Muay Thai, I even emailed one of the website owners asking him:

"Bro, what the fuck man, how could you give Island Muay Thai a good review, you very well know that gym sucks."

He responded, "yeah I know, but this is Thailand, you have to remain politically correct."

This is exactly why it's hard to trust any reviews about gyms. The other reviews on forums are by guys that never trained at any other gym so they have nothing to compare it against. They had a good time at Island Muay Thai mostly because Koh Tao is a fun island to live on. Hopefully one day the trainers will develop their love for Muay Thai again and step up their training, but until then, I cannot recommend Koh Tao's Island Muay Thai to anyone.
There is also another small "muay thai" gym on Koh Tao near the main pier. It's indoors and really tiny, I checked it out one day but was instantly turned off when the instructor explained their colored belt ranking system to me. What I've always loved about Muay Thai is that they focused on what actually works and didn't have stupid colored belts like Karate and Taekwondo have, that you earn by wasting your time memorizing hypothetical katas and forms. I would not recommend this place either to anyone. The only colored belt system that I actually respect is the one in Brazilian Jiu-Jitsu, for all other Martial Arts it's just a way to make you think you're improving so they can keep you as a student and make more money.

Koh Phangan:
I trained at Arena Gym in Koh Phangan a few times on different trips to the island. It is situated in the heart of the full moon party beach, Haad Rin. The gym itself is okay, and is overlooking a lake. The bags were extremely soft and there wasn't any group sessions, only one on one classes. The pad work was okay, but nothing special. I would only recommend this gym if you happen to be staying in Haad Rin anyways for the full moon party and wanted to get a workout in or kick some bags while you are there.
I also checked out Jungle gym, also in the Haad Rin area of Koh Phangan but it's more of a weight lifting gym that also offers some Muay Thai on the side, I didn't train there.

If you want to live and train in Koh Phangan, I would recommend you train in the Thong Sala area, which is the main town, about a 30 minute drive from the full moon party beach. It's only a 100 baht ($3.33US) shared taxi ride to the party so don't risk drinking and driving on a motorbike to go to the party, it's not worth it and would be stupid to do so. The three gyms I would consider are Diamond Muay Thai, Korba, and Muay Thai Chinnarach. Kobra has it's own stadium which is always a good thing if you plan on actively fighting while you're there. Chinnarach recently tore down their own gym and built a brand new one a few blocks away, and Diamond has decent reviews. Since they are all pretty close to each other near the main pier, I would personally get a random hotel for a few nights, rent a motorbike and train one day at each one before making my decision on what the best gym in Koh Phangan is. I've actually considered living and training in Koh Phangan simply because it is such a cool island.

The monthly full moon parties are seriously the best parties in the world, and there are smaller jungle parties every other week. But personally, I think it would be fun to train all month as the island is completely dead 25 days out of the month, and then go all out for 2 or 3 days to let off some during the full moon. I wouldn't even go down to the party on the night of the full moon itself as it gets too hectic and crazy. The parties on the two nights before would be just fine. I could also work as a divemaster part time as the nearby Sail Rock is a good advanced dive site near Koh Phangan.

Koh Samui:
Koh Samui's private airport is possibly the nicest airport in the world, at least out of the 50 or so I've seen in my life. You don't even feel like you're in an airport, it literally feels like you're in a really nice hotel resort. It is a far better than the airport in Hawaii which people often assume would be tropical and beautiful but obviously they've never been to Thailand.

One of the gates at Koh Samui Airport

The entire island is made up of older wealthier tourists and honeymoon couples instead of young backpackers. It's definitely not as much of a party island, but since both Koh Phangan and Koh Tao are so cheap and easy to go to, it's a good hub to train at. The ferry to the neighboring islands of Phangan and Tao will cost 300-500 baht ($10-$16US) are are nice easy boat rides on large comfortable ferries.

Even though Koh Samui is the most expensive of the three islands, living costs are still a bit cheaper than Phuket if you find local places. You can also pitch in with a few friends and rent a luxury villa if you don't mind spending a bit of cash for something that would be double the price back home. A very nice two bedroom house can be found from 36,000 baht ($1,200US) a month. Yet you can still find basic studio apartments for around 5,000 baht ($166US) a month, which what I normally opt for.

Koh Samui has some very nice beaches, but unfortunately because of all of the beach front development, all of the surrounding coral around the island has been covered with sand and is now dead. Also the main port town is quite dirty from all of the fisherman docking up there. I've personally seen them throw plastic bags full of trash straight into the water off the pier. But fortunately, most of the rest of the island is really clean and nice. The biggest problem with Koh Samui are the type of tourists that go there. You get a lot of rude, high end tourists, that treat the local Thais like they are below them, which makes the Thai's in turn be rude back and often see foreigners only as a walking dollar sign.

There are a couple Muay Thai gyms in Koh Samui, from what I heard, the best gym is Jun Muay Thai. They also have really good prices for both accommodation and training. You can get a basic fan room to yourself for 5,500 baht a month and training once a day is only 3,000 baht ($100US) per month! Two a day training is 5,000 baht ($166US) per month. I've always thought that this should be the normal and fair price for Muay Thai in Thailand. But it seems like almost all gyms charge way more.

The other two gyms in Koh Samui that I would check out are Wech Pinyo Muay Thai which seems like it might be a good basic thai style gym and Superpro Samui which seems decent as well, and is the only gym that also offers MMA. I would also check out Lamai Muay Thai which is the gym that is affiliated with the World Muay Thai council and the TV show, the Challenger. Lamai is the gym a lot of Russians train at.

Chiang Mai:
Last but not least, we have my current and new favorite place in Thailand to train. Honestly, I don't know if I would recommend Chiang Mai as the destination for first timers to Thailand. I'm sure you'll still have a good time here, but white sand beaches and nice tropical islands are a huge part of Thailand that isn't up in Chiang Mai. The reason why I can enjoy it so much up here is because I got all of that out of my system first.

There's still plenty to do in Chiang Mai, you can ride a bicycle everywhere, go on 1 to 3 day hikes in the beautiful mountains, and enjoy lunch on a bamboo hut right on top of the lake. There's also a river that runs though the city, and really nice swimming pools to lounge by and top up your tan. My favorite part of Chiang Mai however are the people. There is literally zero bullshit here, and everyone is friendly and no one tries to rip you off. In Phuket and Koh Samui everyone is rude and over charges for things like taxi cabs. In Bangkok, people will try to scam you. But in Chiang Mai, people are friendly and whatever price their quote you for a taxi ride is usually spot on and at most it'll be 50 baht ($1.66US) too high.

In Phuket to the cost of a Taxi from the airport to the road where Tiger Muay Thai and Phuket Top Team are at, the taxi drivers will try to charge you up to 1,300 baht ($43.33US) you they have to haggle and argue to get it down to 600 baht ($20US). While in Chiang Mai, you won't even have to negotiate, the price will be 150 baht. ($5US) Right away, from the moment you step off the plane you will be paying a lot less money, and more importantly, not stressing out as much either. Even taking taxis around town are a pleasant experience with most shared rides being only 20 baht (Less than $1) and having a private taxi take you 30 minutes away for 150 baht ($5).

Rooms and accommodation are also cheaper in Chiang Mai, you can get a basic fan room for as little as 2,500 baht per month ($83US) and for 6,000 baht ($200US) you can live in the city center in a nice place with a swimming pool, air conditioning, wifi, a fridge, TV, cleaning service, elevator, and security. I'm currently paying 4,000 baht ($133US) including utilities, wi-fi, and linen service. One a week I get freshly laundered bath towels, sheets, and pillowcases for free. I can also drop off my laundry next door for 30 baht a kilo ($1US for 2.2lbs of laundry) My room in Chiang Mai is by far the nicest room I've stayed at anywhere in Thailand, and also the cheapest. In Phuket I'd have to share a bathroom and have a smaller place for the same price.

There are a few really good gyms in Chiang Mai, if you want to do MMA your choices are Team Quest and the new Tiger Muay Thai in Chiang Mai. TMT Chiang Mai is huge, literally a sports campus on 7 acres of land which is 28,328 sq. meters in the Mae Rim area. It's a 40-60 minute drive from the actual city of Chiang Mai which is fantastic for dedicated training. There are currently 34 budget rooms being built and expected to be 68 total when they finish. I think TMT coming to Chiang Mai will be a good thing for the gym's reputation. It's the opposite of a party town, especially being so far north of the city, so people will actually train and not just get drunk and chase girls every weekend. I would recommend Tiger Muay Thai Chiang Mai for those who are coming to Thailand and want to dedicate to training and nothing else. If you get bored you can always split a taxi or ride your motorbike into town on weekends and get a hostel for 120 baht a night ($4US).

Edit: Tiger Muay Thai Chiang Mai has closed due to a land dispute with the Thai owners. For more information you can read about it on my blog at www.MyFightCamp.com

Team Quest is the first MMA gym in Chiang Mai and is in an ideal location of the city. It's opposite Central Airport Plaza mall which is where the cinema, shopping and food courts are located, and is a really quick, 5-10 minute drive from the city center. If you want to do MMA but want to be in the city itself, I would recommend Team Quest.

As for Muay Thai only gyms, there are a few good ones to choose from in Chiang Mai. I'm currently at KC Muay Thai and am really happy here. It's a 20 minute drive from the city center, in a very quite countryside town of Mae-Hia but within walking distance I have a Big C Supermarket (think Super-Walmart), a bunch of small Thai restaurants, including one opposite the new Urbana 2 condos with a Thai lady that speaks really good English, making it choice of most guys at the gym. Typical dishes there are 35-40 baht but you can ask for super sized, double meat dishes with two eggs for around 80 baht. ($2.66US) The head trainer Chon is world class fighter and coach and a very genuine, good, honest person and is the reason why I love KC Muay Thai so much. However, one of the main reasons why KC is such a good gym is because it doesn't have a website and very few people come here, literally only through word of mouth. Unfortunately, if KC starts getting really busy, I'm afraid it won't be as good. The gym normally has around 5-10 people training at any given time and can support up to 15. Anything more than that would cause the training to suffer, especially since there is only room for one boxing ring.

Burklerk Gym is in the heart of the city, on the second floor of the night market. It's a bit too busy of an area, and is an indoor gym. Burklerk Pinsinchai is well known to be a world class trainer that speaks good English and has excellent technique. Because of the gym's location, it caters mostly to random tourists that come in for a day or two, and Burklerk isn't often there. If you really want to train with him, email them ahead of time to ask about his schedule. muaythaisiam@hotmail.com He is often at his other gym in Lampang, which is 4 hours away from Chiang Mai. Honestly, I would only train there if I was already in peak cardio conditioning, had a ton of fights, and wanted to take some 1 on 1 private lessons with Burklerk himself to learn some new techniques. For 1 on 1 private lessons, Burlerk would be your best choice followed by Chon at KC or one of the Thai trainers that you get along with at the other gyms.

Lanna and Chay Yai Gym area both close to the city center and popular, but a bit too crowded for my tastes. I've heard mixed reviews for both gyms. So your experience could be good, but it's not my top choice.

Sangha Muay Thai is 20 minutes out of the city, but is more of a meditation, spirituality, and traditional martial arts gym. I'd say it's better than learning Kung Fu or Karate but honestly, it's not my thing and do not recommend it. I'd rather train the basics, foundation, and how to fight at a normal Muay Thai gym. Santai Muay Thai is a bit outside of the city, around 30-40 minute drive away from the city but is located inside a very nice, peaceful countryside. They have a nice Fairtex ring and equipment and a decently good sized gym. What I respect most about Santai is even though the gym can get busy, they pride themselves on quality of training over profits and have actively turn away students once they reach their capacity of 30. What I really like about Santai also is that everyone eats together Thai style, and there seems to be a very good social life at the gym. Overall, I would pick Santai as the best Muay Thai gym in Chiang Mai for most people.

Other Random Places and Gyms:
One of the readers of the first edition of the book asked about a few obscure random gyms that I've never been to, but here are my responses to his question just for everyone's reference.

Emerald Gym in Krabi - I can't speak of the gym itself as I haven't trained there but the area is very good. I really like Krabi as it's less touristy than Phuket by far, but it's still easily accessible. The tourists there are more families and older couples than young backpacker types. You are a short boat ride away from Railey beach though which is famous for young backpackers that come to rock climb, smoke weed and chill on the beach.

KYN in Koh Yao Noi is on a Muslim Island, so there will be very little partying and drinking. Which may be a good thing, it'll be nice to be on an island that isn't popular yet. But it may be boring. I haven't heard anything about the training.

The new Rawai is Khao Lak should be good, at the time of writing they haven't finished construction yet, and sometimes it's bad to go before all the bugs are fixed as there won't be many sparring partners in the start and things like accommodation may have problems.   However Khao Lak is a great area north of

Phuket, quite, nice beach and great scuba diving as it is close to the similan islands.

Getting ripped off for training – Why you might be overpaying.
At home, you would most likely pay around $120US per month of unlimited training. In many parts of Europe, including Holland and Sweden training is often only $60US a month. Why in the world would you pay 10,000 baht ($333US) per month in Thailand where everything else is so cheap? I try to keep quite about this sensitive subject publicly, but in this book, it's no holds barred. You are fucking getting ripped the hell off if you are paying 10,000 baht a month for training. The only reason why gyms in Thailand are able to get away with it is because once you factor in the costs of food and accommodation, your monthly budget is still really low compared to what it would be back home. You also get things like 1 on 1 pad work and more personal time with top quality trainers that you would back home. While most gyms back home only have 1 trainer per class and you hold pads for each other, it's the norm in Thailand to have 1 trainer for every 3 students maximum. The classes are also longer, and you train more often in Thailand than you do at home as well.

So if you think about it logically, paying 10,000 baht a month, or 8,000 baht at Muay Thai only gyms isn't that big of a price tag for training twice a day six days a week. If you do the math, you get 48 sessions per month, and if you do Yoga or Circuit training for a 3rd session in the day, you might even get 60 sessions in! So doing the math, you're really only paying 208 baht ($7US) per session if you train twice a day. That's a fantastic deal. However, that's where reality comes in. I've now trained at more than seven different Muay Thai and MMA gyms across Thailand often for up to 6 months at a time and have seen literally hundreds of students pass through them. Each and every single one of them came with the intention of training twice a day, six days a week. Each and every single one of them, ended up missing 40-60% of their classes by the end of the month. Even pro fighters that come for a fight camp end up getting sick, injured, or simply overworked and become too tired to train.

If you think you are the exception and want to pay for the unlimited monthly membership, go ahead, it's not my money. For some smaller gyms such as KC you're actually helping them out as a lot of the money goes to sponsering young Thai kids go to school and train. But do yourself a favor and keep track of how many days you actually train and how many sessions total you go to. I would happy wager the price of this book against anyone who thinks they will attend even close to 48 sessions in a month. The easiest way to keep track, and what I personally do, is hang up a calendar on the wall and write in what I did everyday. Go ahead and pay for unlimited training for the first month, then tally up how many sessions you actually went to and do the math.

Since I live at the gym at every camp, I go there every single session even if I'm not training, just to stretch, shadow box, do light weights, eat, hang out, say hello, and watch. I see who trains and who doesn't. It also forces me to not get lazy. The worst thing for people that don't live at the gym in regards to training is being able to disappear for weeks at a time without anyone noticing. Most people end up doing the following:

Week 1:
The first two days after arriving, they train twice a day and jump right into things. On the third day, their muscles are so sore and their body aches so much they take a few sessions off and start training once a day. By the fifth day, they still show up for one session but are only able to train at 50% because their feet are blistered up, their shin bones hurt, and their whole body is sore.

Week 2:
During the second week they are committed to training hard twice a day, but are exhausted by Wednesday. They start looking for supplements, protein powder and other things to refuel. Nothing helps. They come to terms and say decide to only train twice a day a few days a week and "rest" by taking a morning off once in a while.

Week 3:
Over the weekend, they discovered all of the amazing things to do in Thailand, then got drunk. They wonder why their carido isn't improving and don't realize it's because their drunken binge over the weekend offset an entire week of training gains. They're also over trained and are physically exhausted. But they continue to push as they promised themselves they would give it their all.

Week 4:
They decide to skip a few of training to further recover, it gets extended to a week and we don't see them again as they are too embarrassed to start up again and are mad at themselves for wasting their money. Total sessions actually attended, twenty nine.

Still when you think about it, training twenty nine times in one month is very impressive. Most people back home only go to the gym a few times a week and even then, those workouts are a piece of cake compared to what we do here in Thailand. Honestly, that's considered a dedicated guy and that doesn't include injury which happens to everyone to a certain degree. If you keep track of how many sessions you actually train at in a month, it might actually be closer to twenty if you factor the days you'll miss from being sick, or recovering from a minor injury.

Like everyone else, I always paid for unlimited training sessions at every gym I went to. And like everyone else, I ended up paying way too much and not using all of my sessions, which by the way, are non-refundable. Now I pay for 10 sessions at a time, and it has saved me thousands of baht every month. Most gyms will let you buy 10 sessions for 2,500 – 3,000 baht. ($83 - $100US) A lot of gyms discourage it as it's a pain in the ass for them to keep track of, but remember, you're the customer and even if you're not on a tight budget, it's still a good idea to not waste money. On average, you will realistically train 20-25 sessions in a month even if you come with the best intentions as most people do. Other things like holidays, visa runs, and hooking up with a girl cause you to miss a few days or ever an entire week sometimes. At the end of the day, 10,000 baht buys you 40 sessions anyway, and I can almost guarantee you won't go over that. Of course you may actually be the exception, but 95% of you will save a lot of money by paying for 10 sessions at a time. Just make sure you keep track and be honest to yourself and to your gym by keeping track accurately.

Johnny FD

If you do go for the unlimited training package, the gym will happy to take your money. First it's easy for them to keep track of what day it expires, second if you do go everyday twice a day, they'll be super proud of you, and third if you stop coming as most people do, they still made money off of you so they don't care. Tiger Muay Thai in Phuket went under a lot of fire for charging people 27,000 baht upfront for three months of training, knowing very well that half of those people will stop coming after a month when they discover the nightlife and girls of Patong or get into a scooter accident on the way back. Most gyms have a strict no refund for any reason policy. At the end of the day, it's your money, but personally it's saved me on average of 3,000 baht a month since I switched and I actually train more often and harder now than I did before when I was on the unlimited plan.

Gym Discounts:
Before I switched over the 10 sessions at a time method, I would try to get discounts on unlimited training. The only ways to get a discount on training are to either, add some type of value to the gym or go when they desperately need to fill spots. Different ways to add value include, being a pro fighter and fighting for the gym or being so famous that just the fact that you're there promotes the gym. If you're not famous, you can have a popular blog or website like I do. It helps promote the gym whenever you write about your experiences there. Other ways include being a decent videographer or photographer and helping film the gym's fights, and making promo videos. If you have web skills you can help update or create their website. By adding value to the gym, most owners are happy to give you a discount on training. Every gym that I trained at offered me half off of unlimited training which was a savings of 5,000 baht ($166US) because of my blog, website, and video making skills.

Honestly, I would have promoted the gyms regardless of if they gave me a discount or not, since my blog was a personal hobby anyways. Even the gym tours and promo videos I made were all just for fun and because I wanted to help out, not because I was ever required to. Not until this book did I ever even consider making a living from my website. But because of my videos Phuket Top Team has gotten 33,926 views on youtube so far, showing potential students what the gym looks like and what the training is like.

Tiger Muay Thai has gotten thousands of potential students from reading about my experiences at the gym on my blog, and guys that decided to go to TMT because of it. KC Muay Thai got their gym name promoted to the 8,751 who have watched Mirkko's fight this month alone and saw that he's training here. Basically, any gym I train at, I do so because I like it there. If I think a gym sucks, I go somewhere else. Therefore, if I'm somewhere for 3 months and it's good, I recommend it to others, which is something I always happily did for free. Then I discovered that even with the 50% discount, it was still often cheaper for me to pay for 10 classes at a time. Plus I get to be a paying student and have no financial ties to any gym, which is a good thing.

Fighting Muay Thai in Thailand – Everything you want to know.
After my first fight in Koh Lanta, I found out that I didn't have to pay for training anymore. I officially became a sponsored fighter, even though I was completely a newbie and wasn't very good. But luckily, the gym owner was also

the stadium owner, so he was happy to waive the price of training in order for me to rematch against the legendary Big Boom, whom I lost to in my first match. At Tiger Muay Thai, after I fought for them and won by knockout, they asked me to stay longer and fight more. When Ray Elbe found out I started training at Phuket Top Team, he asked me to come back,

> "Whatever deal Boyd is giving you--I'm willing to match--I already told Minimac to contact you and make sure $$$ wasn't the reason you were choosing PTT over TMT."

I seriously thought about it, it would have been a great opportunity to become a sponsored fighter at Tiger Muay Thai, but to be honest, I just didn't want anyone to have control over me and I didn't want to owe anyone, anything. One of the stipulations of being a sponsored fighter anywhere is having to train twice a day six days a week and also completing a daily running program. Personally, I like training and recovering on my own pace and don't think it would be best for me, my body or even my fight career. So my advice to you is, even though it sounds like an amazing opportunity to become a sponsored fighter, if you can afford it, it's better to keep your freedom and do it and pay your own way.

When do you know you're ready for your first fight:
The short answer is, your trainer will ask you to fight. Since you'll be representing the gym and his coaching, he doesn't want you to lose, so if he's asking you, you're most likely ready. However, being prepared mentally is completely different.
If you can run 5km in around 30 minutes or so and then complete a Muay Thai workout including 3 rounds of pad work and 3 rounds of sparring, then you are most likely physically ready. I also do the burpee pyramid test which I talked about the previous section about how to prepare before you come to Thailand. To be mentally ready however you really need to spar hard and often. I suggest you spar at 80% with big 16oz gloves but treat it as a real fight, if you get rocked, cover up and continue. If you see your opponent starting to fade, turn on the pressure. You need to be able to recognize when to finish and fight and have the will to do so. You also need to mentally be prepared to be hit hard, injured, exhausted and to keep fighting. It's no joke. Sometimes, especially in Phuket, you might get an easy fight, but it can also be the toughest thing you've ever done in your life and you need to be ready to face it.

How to avoid fighting a Taxi driver that may take a fall on purpose.
A lot of people talk about fighting Tuk Tuk (taxi) drivers. It happens a decent amount since Muay Thai is an easy way for poor Thai guys to make a bit of extra money. Also there are fights 3-5 nights a week and they need to fill opponent spaces. Also think about it this way, if it's your first fight, no one knows who you are, and the promoters have no idea how to match you up, so they just give you anyone. The best way to assure you get legitimate fights is to prove yourself first. Instead of fighting once just to say you did, plan on having a fight every 2-3 weeks while you are in Thailand. I guarantee that once the promoters see you they will better match you up for the next fight.

The reason why a lot of Thai opponents will take falls is because they get paid the same whether they win or lose, but don't think they won't knock you out if they have the chance. All of my fights have been against Thai guys, and they have all tried to knock me out or at least cut me with elbows. The last guy I fought took a fall in the second round. I'm not 100% sure, but I'm pretty sure he could have gotten up and taken an eight count instead. But one thing is for sure, he knocked some of my teeth loose and broke my nose with elbows, and I in turn, punched and kicked him with everything I had trying to knock him out. Even though he didn't get up after the knee in the second round, don't think for a second that he wouldn't have knocked me out if he had the chance. It's a lot easier for them to just knock you out in the first round than to take a fall. I'm pretty sure the reason why he didn't get up is because he knew I was determined to win, and he would have faced exhaustion and possible injury if he got up. Another way to avoid getting a tuk-tuk driver is to ask to fight another farang, which is what Thais call foreigners. The problem however with fighting another Western guy is it'll most likely turn into a brawl with no technique. For beginner fights, it always ends up being a one sided boxing match whenever two farangs are involved. Sometimes it's also hard for them to find another non-thai person to match up against you, which is why most first fights are against Thai people. I'd suggest fighting Thai guys for your first few matches and then fighting a fellow farang.

Here in Chiang Mai, I was really surprised that the fights were a bit more serious but the stadiums were a lot more shitty. Overall the quality of fights have been much better in Chiang Mai and even for people's first fights they have been matched up with really good opponents that are just as determined to win as they are. I think the reason is because up in the north, Thai fighters are trying to make a career out of it as they are poor. They really want to win and have a good record so they can move up to Lumpinee stadium in Bangkok one day. The fighters in Chiang Mai are hungry and want to win and I haven't seen any take a fall on purpose since I've been here.

The bad news about Chiang Mai however is you get paid a lot less, and you don't get a cool fight poster with your face on it to take home. The good thing however is you get good experience, and your friends can go watch your fight fr 300 baht ($10US) instead of 1,000 ($33US) that they charge in Phuket. Finally after two months of training here in Chiang Mai, I finally feel fit and ready to take a fight. It'll be my fifth fight in Thailand but I'm a tiny bit nervous because I haven't fought in 18 months. After my last fight with Mailai my teeth were a bit loose and I couldn't even spar for 6 months. Then I took on a full time job teaching scuba diving in Borneo where they didn't have Muay Thai. And finally I spent the summer in America which made me take a while to get back into shape.

My plan is to fight at 95kg (209lbs) two weeks from now even though I'm 217lbs right now. Hopefully I'll have a semi-easy win and not get any injuries so I can ask for another fight straight away and keep up the streak as long as I can. My second goal is to walk around at 93kg (202lbs) and eventually fight at 85kg (187lbs). Ideally I'll be able to fight once every two weeks while I'm here and bang out as much experience as I can during this fight camp. In Chiang Mai you only get 2,000 - 2,500 baht per fight instead of the normal 5,000 baht ($166US) I'm used to in Phuket and Koh Lanta. But the nice thing is the gyms in Chiang Mai don't take a cut, although tipping your corner men 500 is appropriate and appreciated. At Tiger Muay Thai, I received around 2,500 baht after the trainers

Johnny FD

and gym took their 20% of 5,000. Maybe my math isn't very good or maybe both the gym and the trainer takes 20% each, but at the end of the day, I ended up with around half of what it said on the envelope.

To sign up to fight, simply ask your trainer. In Thailand, it's normal to have fights 1-2 weeks out, so make sure you are ready the day you ask. The promoter will come and take your photo and possibly weigh you in. In Phuket I never got weighed in at all, but here in Chiang Mai they do, although it's still not super strict and no one cuts water weight the day before the fight for these small matches, only for fights with a lot of money on the line. The nice thing about Thailand and one of the reasons why 6 months of training and fighting in Thailand is often considered worth 3 years of training back home is because it's so easy to get fights here.

How to Win your First Professional Fight – and why losing it may actually be better in the long run.
This next part I wrote about on my blog, but here it is in an updated and expanded version, if you plan on fighting, read this carefully, it may change the outcome of your fight.

Every time I try to give someone advice on what to do during their first fight, I always get the same response, "yeah yeah yeah, I got this, I already know what to do." On one hand, it's good that they're confident, but I guess if they weren't, they wouldn't have taken a fight in the first place.

But 90% of guys make the same couple mistakes during their first fight and end up losing. Part of me wants to scream at the guy and tell him to fucking listen, and stop being over confident, but at the same time, maybe it's good for people to lose their first fight, that way they can truly be open to learning and better preparing for their second fight.

I wasn't any better, I went into my first fight cocky, arrogant, thinking that it would be easy. I told myself, Thai guys aren't very good at boxing, I'll just out box him. The stupid thing that my friend Nic later pointed out is that it's not like I studied much boxing either. I was lucky, the fight went to decision and I lost. It was then, and only then did I put my ego aside and really want to learn, improve and work hard.

Here are a list of things that can help you win your first fight.

1. **Make sure you have good cardio -**

Five rounds of 3 minutes each is a very very long time once you're in the ring, especially if your adrenaline is pumping and you are tense. If you don't already run, make sure you can run 3 miles (5km) straight without stopping and in around 30 minutes. Another good way to build and test your cardio is with burpees. I do a descending pyramid of burpees with a pushup. Basically you would start by squatting down, jumping back into a pushup position, doing a single pushup, jumping back into squat, and then finishing by jumping straight in the air before repeating the process. Start with 12 burpees, rest for 30 seconds, do 11 burpees, rest 30 seconds, then 10 rest, 9, rest, 8, rest, 7, rest, 6, rest, 5, rest, 4, rest, 3, rest, 2, rest, 1, rest. If you can get through the entire pyramid with good form, you just did a total of 55 burpees, and you've passed the cardio test. The best thing about this is it's a full body workout that you can do anywhere without any gym equipment.

Jumping rope is also good for developing good cardio, rhythm and a bounce in your step. Get yourself a weighted jump rope if you do.

2. **Spar a lot then Rest a lot -**

The most important thing you can do before your fight is spar a lot, you can look amazing on the pads but if you never spar, it'll show in the ring. Mix it up with Muay Thai sparring, boxing sparring and clinch sparring to get used to all three, but try to do Muay Thai Sparring most often as that's what you'll be fighting.

Also remember that fighting cardio is different from running cardio. I've met guys that can run 10km easily but get exhausted in the ring after two rounds because they are too tense and not relaxed. Sparring a lot teaches you how to get a rhythm down so you can explode when needed and conserve energy at other times.

If you're going to be fighting MMA, make sure you work a lot on your wrestling, take down defense and getting off your back. You can't learn Brazilian Jiu-Jitsu in 3 weeks before your fight but you can learn how to avoid getting put on your back and how to stand if you do you. Do a lot of sprawls if you're going to be fighting MMA, literally do 100 sprawls after every practice, especially when you are tired and don't want to do it, that's when you're gonna get taken down. Even better have a friend shoot in on you while you sprawl to make it more realistic. When you spar, make sure you time it for 3 or 5 minutes, the same as your fight and don't stop half way to adjust your gear or talk. Treat the pace like a real fight and learn how to get out of bad positions, or out of the corner in Muay Thai. 48-72 hours before your fight, stop training and do nothing. Rest and relax. Stay out of the sun, don't run, you'll need the energy for your fight. You can shadow box and think about technique and strategy and try to watch a lot of beginner fights on youtube. Watching high level pros isn't going to help you much aside from motivation, but watching others people's first fights and seeing their mistakes may help you not make the exact same ones.

This is a huge advantage you can get that no one ever does. Everyone wants to imitate Anderson Silva, Jon Bones Jones, Masato, or Buakaw, but as a beginner you are much better off watching youtube videos of random guy's first fights, especially if they lose. Analyze the fights and ask yourself what you would have done differently in each situation, and more importantly, how he could have finished the fight.

3. **Be prepared to get hit and cover up -**
It's funny that a lot of guy don't actually realize they're in a fight until the first hard shot they take. Then the realize that it isn't just fun and games, the guy in the ring is trying to kill you. Make sure you check his kicks, you'll be surprised

how many guys don't check kicks until it's too late. The first few low kicks to your thigh may not hurt too much, but trust me, eventually it'll make your leg numb and want to collapse, check the fucking kicks. Keep your hands up and watch out for head kicks. During your first fight, often you'll realize what you really signed up for. This is the make it or break it moment for most guys, this is when you either man up or you start making excuses. If you choose the latter, don't think for a second that people won't know you bitched out, they may listen to your excuse and accept it, but deep down inside, they know you bitched out.

Either way, you'll know you bitched out and it will haunt you for the rest of your life.

4. **Punch straight and avoid the clinch and elbows -**
Thai's love to clinch and exchange knees. Don't play their game, you'll lose or at least get seriously hurt. Instead of throwing hooks and other big loopy punches that allow your opponent to step in and clinch you, only throw straight jabs and straight rights. Keep your distance, even if you get the guy on the ropes of in the corner, don't rush in too close or he'll clinch you. Instead, keep at arms length so you can jab and through straight rights without him being able to grab you. Sometimes you'll need to move back while punching.

Also watch out for elbows. It's something that you won't be used to receiving since you never get elbowed during sparring. I used to really love throwing hooks to the body until I received my 4th short elbow to the face. If you're getting elbowed, you need to keep your hands up and go back to straight punches instead of hooks.

5. **Set up your kicks with punches -**
Don't throw super projected kicks, they are a waste of energy. Instead, make your kicks count. If you watch any Muay Thai fight, the first 5 kicks or so are fast and powerful. Then they start slowing down. Set up your kicks with punches, or even fakes. If you're going to kick, commit to it and put some speed and power behind it. Your best bet to beat a Thai guy in his sport is to throw a lot of punches to neutralize his kicks and mix it up with kicks of your own.

Personally, I don't throw kicks for points, every kick I throw is intended to do damage.

6. **Be Aggressive -**
At lower levels, especially with beginners, the guy that is most aggressive usually wins the fight. So move forward, throw lots of straight punches and follow them up with hard kicks. Look for the opportunity to finish the fight. When your opponent is tired, he's going to want a way out, give it to him by being extra aggressive and going for the kill as soon as you see the opportunity arise. If what you're doing isn't working, change it up. In my last fight, I threw tons of hard body kicks and punches that seemed to do nothing so I started throwing knees, which finally ended the fight. Remember that you have 8 limbs and 8 different tools to knock your opponent out with, and everyone has a weakness, exploit it.

7. Finish the fight - Never leave it to the judges

If you don't finish the fight and get a bad decision, it's your fault. Especially in Muay Thai rules, the person that does the most damage or looks like they should have won, often doesn't. Things like most punches and low kicks don't score points. While knees in the clinch, even if they don't do any damage, score lots of points. You have 5 rounds to KO or TKO your opponent. If you are aggressive and seize the chances to overwhelm him, you can finish the fight. If you don't and it goes to decision, it's no one's fault but your own. Leave it all in the ring, as long as you came into the fight with decent cardio, realize that he's just as tired as you are. The worst thing you can do for the audience and for yourself when you look back on the fight is to stall and wait for the decision. You will regret it, and everyone will know you were a bitch for doing so. Leave it all in the ring and go for the finish each and every time.

8. Your first fight in 80% Mentality -

Especially with beginners, the guy that has the most heart, the one that truly wants to kill his opponent and leave it all in the ring usually wins. At higher levels having heart and a good mentality can only take you so far if you're being out classed with technique, but in the lower levels of fighting, it goes a very long way. Ask yourself how badly you really want it and if you are fit to be a fighter. Not everyone is, and excuses don't make anyone feel better but yourself. For me personally, I wasn't mentally or physically prepared for my first fight.
My cardio was lacking from not running, and I didn't have the killer instinct. Luckily, my opponent accepted a rematch and I ended up beating him the second time around. After losing my first fight to decision, I stepped up my training by training by running everyday after class. Technique wise I made myself only jab and throw straight punches to avoid the clinch, and I went for the knock out, which I got in the second round.

What to eat before your fight:

The night before your fight you want to load up on some carbs, sweet potatoes would be your best choice if you can find them, followed by white rice. On the day of your fight, don't eat anything too spicy or anything suspect. Try to eat what you would normally eat on a training day. Eat your last meal 4 hours before your fight, however, realize that even though the fights are scheduled to start at 9pm, you might not be fighting until closer to eleven as often they put the foreigners as the main event.
An hour before your fight, you can optionally drink half a redbull, for that extra push from the sugar and caffeine.

What bring to your fight:

The stadium and your trainer will provide most things such as the gloves, hand wraps, and metal cup. You need to bring your mouth guard and Muay Thai shorts. Make sure you wear underwear under your shorts since they'll need to put the cup on last minute before your fight. I didn't and it was a bit embarrassing. I also suggest wearing a sweatshirt to keep you warm before the fight and bring some music to listen to. You'll often have a few hours of downtime before you actually fight and you want something to keep the nerves down. It's also a good idea to bring a pair of flip flops to walk to the ring in as it'll be hard to put on normal shoes with gloves on.

Filming your fight:
Bring an experienced camera man. You'll regret not having proper video of your fight if you don't. Have him take a few photos for you before the fight and more importantly film the entire fight. Have him stand on the corner of the ring, on top of the actual ring and not from the ground or the crowd. Filming from the audience stands requires zooming which makes the picture shaky. Sometimes it's worth the money to hire a pro. I've seen inexperienced guys miss entire rounds thinking they were recording when they weren't, and I've seen it more than once. I've also seen some really shitty filming from the audience stands. Ask your gym if they have someone that can film for you, the going rate in Phuket was 1,500 baht for filming and editing. If you're asking a friend to film for you, it would be courteous for you to pay for his or her entrance fee. Recently I discovered how cool it is to have a professional photographer take photos of your fight. I was lucky to have my buddy Michael White who runs Muay Thai Photography come to my last two fights. Capturing the moment through a high resolution photo that only a digital SLR camera can do can be a beautiful keepsake photo. Ideally you would have a professional photographer with a DSLR camera and an experienced videographer, even if 100% of your fight purse went to paying these two guys, it would be worth it, trust me, when you're 65 and looking back on your life, you're going to want these memories.

Keep up the fight streak:
One of my biggest regrets is not taking more fights immediately afterward each win. You'll already be in shape, and as long as you're not injured there's no reason why you can't fight a week or two later. Doing so is the best way to get a lot of experience under your belt. For me, I always schedule my fights at the end of a 3 month fight camp right before I'm about to go home. The good thing is, I'm usually really fit and ready by then, but the bad is since I'm leaving I can't fit in another fight before I go. Which is why this time, I'm planning on staying for 6 months, which allows me to start fighting at the end of three months, and be able to squeeze in a few more over the next three months before I go home. Perfect.

Fighting MMA in Asia – How to get MMA fights in China, Malaysia, Philippines and Thailand
You can easily get both K-1 style and MMA fights throughout Asia if you are a foreigner and in good shape, you just need a hookup. MMA in Asia is getting huge and one thing that every fight promoter is looking for is international variety. Having fighter's from all around the world on their cards make the productions look prestigious and exciting. Imagine if OneFC only had Malaysia vs Malaysia fights, or SFL (Super Fight League) only had India vs. India, no one would watch their fights. The same goes in China, their ideal card would be filled with China vs. USA, China vs. England, China vs. Japan, and obviously they would want to win, but at the end of the day, it's still up to you.

Even as a beginner, as long as you are from a foreign country and are willing to fight, you'll find a fight somewhere if you look around. The best places to find fights are through facebook. Like as many MMA gym's pages as you can so you can get updates. I get "Fighter's Wanted" posts at least once a month on my feed. After that you can email owners of gyms. All MMA gym owners have some type of hookup to fight productions. Obviously, if you are in the area, get to know the gym owners in person and try to train out of a gym that has connections. But even if you're doing it online, just send them 3 photos, your record/experience, weight class(es), height, age, style, and location. The most important factor for getting MMA Fights in other countries would be your location and how cheap they can fly you into their country for. One of the good things about Phuket and Bangkok, is it's relatively cheap for the promoters to fly you to China, Philippines, Singapore and Malaysia. If the need to fly you from the U.S.A. or Canada, they won't do it unless you already have a big name. If you are willing to travel on your own money, tell the gym owners to pass that info along and chances are you'll get a lot of fights. The other two ways to get fights is to get to know fighters and promoters directly.

Simply hanging out with Will "the kill" Chope got me offers without me even looking for them. I wasn't ready to fight MMA but got offered a fight in China against an English boxer so I figured it'd be boxing verses Muay Thai mainly so I took it. I've done a bit of Brazilian Jiu-Jitsu and Wrestled throughout high school so I figured even though I haven't been training for MMA, I'd do it just for the experience. What I learned from that however is until you get a contract it's just talk. The English guy ended up backing out and they found two different fighter's in a lower weight class to fill the spot. Going to shows as a part of fighter's entourage or being their corner men also help you meet fight promoters. I have a couple added on my facebook now that put up blasts once in a while looking for fighters.

Chapter 6: Tempting things you really should avoid.

Steroids, EPO and HGH – Who uses them, how to get them, and why you shouldn't do them.

I always knew steroids played a big part in professional sports, but it wasn't until I started getting to know some professional fighters that I found out how many people actually use them. It turns out that at the really high levels of sports everyone, literally everyone with the exception of 1% use something or have used something. But most people don't use steroids for what you would think.

Aside from looking tougher, using steroids to bulk up for Muay Thai or MMA is counter productive. It may make you stronger but it also hurts your cardio and gives your calves crazy pumps when you are trying to run. Having big muscles puts you up a weight class, when the idea is to fight at the lowest weight you can, and it can make you slower and less flexible if you get huge. So why in the world would pro athletes use them? They use it mainly for recovery. By doing Steroids and HGH you can recover from those harsh two a day workouts much faster, which ultimately makes you faster, stronger, and have better technique since you're training more often. Fighter's also never use steroids while they fight, only during off seasons and during training.

There is however a drug called EPO (erythropoietin), which is getting more and more popular in MMA and the UFC because it gives you virtually unlimited cardio. The way it works is it increases your body's red blood cells so you have more oxygen in your blood. EPO also helps your body buffer lactic acid, making it so your muscles can preform harder for longer before getting tired. The reason why it's so hard to test for EPO is because there are other ways to get similar benefits without taking oral pills. Some athletes use something called blood doping, where they literally take blood out of their body a month or so before their fight, let your body recover and rebuild it, then transfuse the blood back into their body, giving them more red blood cells than before. Since it is their own blood, it is currently impossible to test for.

The drugs that Lance Armstrong the Tour De France cycle race winner got busted for, would be the same drugs that would benefit fighters. The goal is increased blood cells, cardio, useable muscle, lowering lactic acid, and recovery. Those drugs would be EPO, human growth hormone, testosterone, and anti-inflammatory steroids (cortisone).

Human Growth Hormone (HGH) is a wonder drug. It's literally the closest thing we have to the fountain of youth. HGH is a naturally occurring hormone that we produce mainly while we are sleeping. As a teenager we produce quite a bit of it, especially during puberty, on average around 2.1 iu's (international units) a day. As an adult you produce less and less as you age, and average 1.3 iu's a day as you get into your thirties. Aside from the anti-aging benefits of HGH such as better skin, nails, hair, eye sight, and organ repair, there are direct benefits to sports. HGH increases your body's ability to burn fat and build lean muscle, it repairs joints, and allows your body to recover much better and faster. Remember when you were 20 years old and you could run, have a tough workout, party all night, and then go to work the next day like nothing happened? That's partly because of your body's high HGH levels doing the repair work overnight.

Most high level athletes do a small dose of HGH, around 2iu's a day, which is enough just for recovery. Some bump it up closer to 4iu's a day if they are trying to cut fat and build muscle. Any dose higher than that would be dangerous. If you are going to do HGH make sure you do it during the day at least 3 hours before you go to bed so it doesn't interfere with your body's natural ability to produce the hormone and shut down. Also make sure you cycle it on and off, taking a month off a few times a year. The only reason why I am not doing HGH and why I do not recommend it to others currently is because of cost and authenticity. If you buy HGH from your normal steroid hookup, a pharmacy, or online, you will at best get a diluted form of the drug that may only contain 10% of what it says it does. HGH is currently extremely expensive to manufacture so labs in China that make legitimate pharmaceutical grade HGH also release lower rate product, and unfortunately it's almost impossible to test it's strength. Your 100iu kit may only actually contain 10iu's plus 90iu's of filler.

If I had an actual legitimate, U.S. Pharmaceutical grade prescription from a real doctor, and could afford it, I would do a small does of HGH in a heart beat. The benefits are amazing and the side effects of a small dose are almost non existent. Do not buy HGH in Thailand, even from a Pharmacy. They may swear it's legitimate, and even believe so themselves, but trust me, it's not. Unless you are willing to get it directly from a doctor and pay $600US for a month's supply, hold off on it for a few years until the prices of production come down.

As far as steroids is concerned the best steroid for endurance type athletes including fighters is Testosterone inter-muscular injections. When I researched the topic, Testosterone Ethanate, also known as Test E was the way to go. Most beginners start with 500mg a week, divided into two 250mg doses. However, for endurance sports such as Muay Thai and even things like long distance cycling, 250mg a week is actually enough. I'm sure everyone on the forums will tell you that it's a waste to do such a small dose and that you're an idiot for doing it, but those guys are wrong and most likely don't do Muay Thai, they're body builders. A small dose is great for strength, getting ripped, building some muscle, and most beneficial of all, recovery from hard workouts.

Do it for 12 weeks then have post cycle therapy, known as PCT. Clomid taken after a cycle of steroids will bring your body back to normal and prevent your body from shutting down it's natural testosterone production. If I was ever going to do steroids, I would do a 12 week cycle of Test E, once a week at 250mg, by itself and nothing else.

Or my other option would be going to my doctor and getting put on TRT, Testosterone Replacement Therapy. The only reason why I haven't done testosterone personally is because I just don't feel like I really need it to achieve my current goals. Maybe if I was competing at a super high level and trying to get into the UFC, but as a beginner athlete I want to see what my body's natural potential is first before I start fucking with it. Also it's expensive, even though Testosterone is a lot cheaper than other options, it'll still end costing a few hundred dollars and even the post cycle therapy is expensive. I'd rather spend that money on healthy food, a good lifestyle, massages, and more months in Thailand.

If you really want to do steroids in Thailand anyway, just ask around your gym. Literally just go up to the biggest guy at your gym and ask him. Since steroids are legal in Thailand and you can buy them over the counter in Pharmacies, they should have no problems hooking you up. In Phuket, the Pharmacy next to 711 at the end of the road past Phuket Top Team is where a lot of people I know bought theirs. You can also get it at the Phuket Fight Store. In Bangkok and Pattaya, just go to your local weight lifting gym and go to the closest pharmacy to the gym and they'll have it guaranteed. In Chiang Mai, go to the Pharmacy's that are closest to hospitals. The small random shops won't have things like Test E, but the ones downstairs from a hospital will. Prices in Thailand are comparable to prices in Mexico.

Is using EPO, HGH and Steroids cheating?
Yes and no. I think EPO is cheating for sure, but at the same time, you can develop more red blood cells naturally by living and training at altitude. A lot of fight camps and Olympic training centers are high in the mountains because of this reason. You can also build a high altitude tent in your house to sleep in to get similar results. Devices such as elevation training masks and the Bas Rutten o2 trainer which I'm currently using as I type, also have some benefit, although these are more to make your lungs more efficient than actually raise red blood cells.

I personally don't consider HGH cheating, if anything, it's a way where older athletes such as guys in their late 30's and 40's can still train hard and recover, keeping up with the young kids. As for steroids, because of weight classes, I don't think it's a bad thing for fighting sports. The thing is, even without steroids and other performance enhancing drugs, the playing field is never fair, some people naturally have more testosterone, and better genetics. At the end of the day, just because a guy does steroids doesn't mean he's going to be a good fighter, in fact, often times the big guy that spends too much time lifting weights and not enough time sparring isn't as good. Just look at the K1 fight between Mirko Cro Crop and Bob Sapp for proof.

Recreational Drugs – Weed, Ecstasy, Mushrooms, Opium, and Amphetamines. Thailand now has crazy harsh penalties for drugs but used to be known as destination to come openly do them. Things have changed and fines, bribes and penalties have become even more harsh.

Weed – Where in come from in California, Marijuana is basically legal and it's really not that big of a deal. The same thing goes for smoking weed in certain parts of Thailand. Down in Koh Tao, if you go to the southern part of the island or to any of the reggae bars, you can ask for a joint for 100 baht ($3.33US) Most of the time they are very open about it and you can smoke it in public at the bar, but sometimes they'll flat out say no. Most of it depends on if there are any crackdowns or cops on the island at the time. However, if a cop catches you with weed on you, it's still a big deal and you are looking at paying a large bribe to get out of it.

No one wants to go to jail in Thailand, trust me, or better yet, read one of the many books about how disgusting conditions are in Thai prisons. First thing to do is be really really apologetic and respectful. Put your hands together and bow to the police officer. Pay the bribe if he asks you for one, if he doesn't, ask if you can just fine the fine now in cash, which is a polite way of offering a bribe. It can be as low as 10,000 baht ($333US) or as high as 60,000 baht ($2,000US). If you get taken down to the station, and more cops get involved, they will all want a bribe, multiplying what you'll have to pay.

Mushrooms – The easiest place to get mushrooms are in Koh Phangan at the full moon party. There is a bar on the far end of the beach called Mellow Mountain, where you can get Mushroom Shakes. They are pretty expensive at around 500 baht each and sometimes aren't very strong, but honestly save your money and your mushroom tripping experience for a time you can be somewhere peaceful and quite, maybe camping with friends, than being on a hot sunny beach with 30,000 strangers.

Ecstasy – The perfect drug for the Full Moon Party, it's a shame that MDMA is no longer easily available You can still get it if you know someone, but it's not like it was 10 years ago where the FMP was one big rave. Do not be tempted to buy it off of some random person on the beach, there is a really high chance they will scam you for money or have the police scam you for bribes. Get it through a friend and hide it well. Expect to pay 800 baht ($26.66US) to 1,000 baht ($33US) per pill. MDMA would be a super fun drug to be on at the Full Moon Party, too bad everyone else won't be on it. If you do buy it in Koh Phangan during the party, it would be a good idea to swallow it immediately.

Opium and Heroin – Thailand and the Golden Triangle including Laos and Burma are known for their opiates, and I'm sure twenty years ago during the war, it was very wide spread and easy to get. But honestly, I never hear of anyone in Thailand doing either. In Laos however, up in Viang Vieng where the tubing used to be Opium is openly advertised in menus. I've been offered it a few times but I'm pretty sure it was just weed. Maybe they sprinkled a tiny bit of tar into it or something but I have no idea. Either way, it's definitely not the opium den type of scenario you'd think of.

I did have another friend smoke genuine opium at a shop in Lao and he said it was a decent experience but everyone threw up and got violently ill either that night or the next morning. He said he'd never do it again and it wasn't that fun to begin with.

Amphetamines – Yaba is a mixture of methamphetamine and caffeine, and can be smoked or swallowed in pill form. Almost all bar girls use Yaba and it can be quite easy to get. However, it's also the reason why 90% of people are in Thai prison It's tempting to them during the full moon party, but honestly, I'm so fucking scared of going to prison in Thailand that I won't touch the stuff. Read The Damage Done, Rotting in the Bangkok Hilton, or any of the books written by foreigners that have served time in a Thai prison and you too will stay far far away. You can instead, go to the pharmacy and ask for "diet pills" which are basically the same thing, just make sure you either swallow it immediately or hide it well as I'm not sure how legal they are.

Bar girls, Hookers, and Prostitutes: Why normal guys that would never normally pay for sex, end up doing so in Thailand.
During my time Tiger Muay Thai and to a lesser extent at Phuket Top Team, I've seen a lot of guys, normal guys, who have never paid for sex their entire lives, go down to Patong and fuck a hooker. Some will flat out admit to it, but most guys, will have an excuse on how he didn't pay for sex, or how she isn't really a prostitute.

Most guys will say, and honestly believe, that the girl that brought home, had sex with and gave money to wasn't a hooker.

"Nah, she's not a bar girl, she's only friends with the bar girls. I just gave her some money for taxi fare, that's all."

"She's just in town for a few months, she's a good girl. I just gave her some money because she missed work while hanging out with me"

"Bro, I got it for free, I didn't pay her anything....expect for the 1,000 baht I gave her so her family could buy a new water buffalo."

So why is it that normal guys, ones that could easily get a girl back home pay for sex? It's one thing for old, fat, creepy men with no social skills to do it, but why in the world would a good looking, in shape, young guy fuck a hooker? It's the same reason why men go to McDonald's when they could easily have a steak somewhere else, possibility even for free at home. I honestly think it's because guys are so sick and tired of girls playing games back home that when they discover how cheap and easy it is to hook up with a Thai bar girl, they just give in.

A guy I once met said it best and it's hard not to agree with him,

"I don't go through the hassle of picking up a girl and dating her to have sex with her, if I wanted sex, I would just go pay 1,000 baht ($33US) for sex with a hooker, I go through the madness and jump through girl's hoops because I want a relationship."

It's kind of sad if you think about it. I understand why western girls do what they do, they want to make sure they get the best guy possible, and they want you you to work hard to get them so they feel special and know that you're invested. But at the same time, I understand why that drives most guys nuts and why they are sick of playing those games.

The other thing about Thai bar girls is they're really different from what a prostitute in other parts of the world are like, maybe it's because most of them grew up in small farm towns, or the fact that most of them are in their early twenties, uneducated and immature, or maybe it's because they genuinely are hopeless romantics that are truly hoping to find a nice rich western guy that will marry her and take care of her. The reason why western guys like Thai girls so much, even if they happen to be a bar girl, is because most guys love how caring and nurturing Asian girls are. They really do take care of you, make you feel like a man, cook, clean, and never say no to sex. It's literally like every guys dream. Expect for mine.

Maybe it's because I'm Chinese-American and my first three girlfriends were all Asian. It could be that everyone just wants something different than themselves and to me Thai girls just aren't exotic. Maybe I just really like White girls and their independence. Whatever it is, I'm honestly not that attracted to Thai girls and really don't like the idea of being used for my money, even if it is only 1,000 baht. Even if I get the gir totally for free and never pay for a dime, I still wouldn't want to deal with it the drama. Here's a tip, never give a Thai bar girl your phone number. She'll call you randomly at 4am all of the time, usually she's drunk or on something else and wants you to come over.
One of the big reasons why I moved to Chiang Mai and got the hell out of Phuket was even though Patong Beach, the red-light district of Phuket is 40 minutes away, it still plays a big part in weekly life at the camp.

I've had my fuel lines in my motorbike cut twice and had a full tank of gas stolen by bar girls that came home with guys at the gym while training at Phuket Top Team. I was advised to only keep a quarter of gas in my tank at all times after that, which was a pain in the ass but still easier than getting my fuel lines redone each week. At Tiger Muay Thai, a guy brought home two bar girls to drink, hang out and party. They slipped him something that knocked him out and proceeded to rob him of all his electronics and money. On their way out the door, they saw his neighbor drinking on the balcony and did the exact same thing to him. The second guy woke up the next morning realizing what had happened and got in a fight with the guy that brought the girls home initially. At the end of the day, they had both gotten robbed and lost everything, having to cut their trip short and go home. I don't trust bar girls and would never want one in my room. If the urge really gets to you and you feel the need to bang one out, don't' bring her home. Go get a soapy massage, or take a girl to a backroom hotel, use a condom, do your thing, and go home.

What I really like about Chiang Mai is that sex tourism is virtually non-existent up here and is definitely not a destination. You might see a couple bar girls here and there but compared to Phuket, Bangkok, and especially Pattaya, Chiang Mai is a very normal city with very normal girls. Out of all of Thailand, if you genuinely want to date a normal Thai girl, Bangkok and Chiang Mai would be the only two places to really do it. Chiang Mai University has tons of college girls that you could meet and potentially date if you hang out where the university students hang out near the Nimmanhaemin district. Or better yet, meet some normal Thai guys and hang out with them. If you go to the tourist areas such as Zoe in Yellow aka "the soi" you'll end up meeting a bunch of bar girls.

Chapter 7: Even more value for your money.

Practical Information: Doing Laundry and Day to Day Life.
A lot of things that aren't covered in this book are simply because they really don't matter right now and they are easy to figure out once you get here. The most important thing isn't trying to plan every little thing before you come, but instead to simply just plan your trip and come.

However a lot of people, especially people coming to train Muay Thai, Brazilian Jiu-Jitsu or MMA ask about laundry so here it is. For general day to day laundry, it is far easier just to drop it off at the front desk of whatever hotel you fare staying at, or down the street at a laundry shop as sometimes it is cheaper. Most places charge between 30 baht ($1US) and 50 baht ($1.57US) a kilo which is 2.2lbs. It's actually cheaper to have someone wash, dry and fold your laundry than it is to use a coin operated laundry machine back home.

As for your Muay Thai Shorts or Jiu-Jitsu Gi, you may want to hand wash it after each training since you'll be using them every day. I made a habit of washing my workout clothes in a bucket with some detergent while taking a shower straight after each workout. I kept a bucket in the shower and would fill it up with soapy water, strip off my workout clothes and let it soak while I showered. When I was done, I would simply rinse everything with clean water until it ran clear. To dry, I would wring it out and hang it to dry. Since Thailand is so hot, Muay Thai shorts typically dry within a few hours and a Gi can dry in a day if it's under the sun.

If you plan on doing a lot of jiu-jitsu while you're here, I would recommend you bring two Gis with you. The other option is to arrange a deal with the laundry girl at your gym to have her wash your Gi for you after every class.
Aside from doing laundry most day to day necessities can be bought at 711. It's a bit funny in the beginning going to 711 for everything, but they are everywhere in Thailand and it's common to go there for everything from buying a Sim card for your phone, topping it up with minutes, paying bills, buying laundry detergent, toothpaste, you name it. Just remember, don't sweat the small stuff, and most of it is small stuff. You'll quickly figure it out by asking around once you get to Thailand.

10 Days of Silent Meditation – 7 Valuable life lessons I learned.

The first time I heard of doing a 10 day silent meditation was after meeting a very unique group of backpackers in Chiang Mai. They all really seemed genuine, and present and happy. I asked them the typical questions, where are you from, how long are you staying in Thailand, where have you been, you know the same old, same old.

However, instead of the normal answers I've heard a hundred times, they blew my mind telling me about what they had just come back from, it was called Vipassana.

"Wait...so you actually lived in a monastery with Buddhist monks for ten days, and you weren't allowed to talk? What did you eat, isn't it hard to meditate? Did you just read all day? Wait, what you're not even allowed to read?"
So it turns out there are these 10 day silent meditation retreats all over Thailand, where you live, eat, sleep, like a monk and meditate all day. It also turns out, that it was one of the hardest things I've ever done in my life, and I've done a lot of crazy things. I've climbed the highest mountain in South East Asia, been scuba diving with sharks, been in four pro Muay Thai fights, but this was hard, really hard, and the only thing I've ever come close to giving up on because of it. I first arrived at Suan Mokk in Suratthani, southern Thailand, mainly because I had no idea other retreats existed. But, it turned out to be the perfect place. The temple is in the middle of a forest, and you meditate around a small lake which in the middle has a tiny island, called nirvana. The retreat starts every month on the last day of the month, I arrived a day before and stayed in the free dorms just to get situated and clear my head before it all started.

The 10 days is more like 12 as it starts on the 30th and ends on the 11th of each month. During those nights, you get your own room but don't expect any luxuries. In fact, one of the ten precepts you'll practice is not sitting or laying on comfortable beds. It took a few nights to get used to my wooden bed, but my back has never felt better afterwards. The wooden pillow however, was a different story.

Ten Precepts
- Refrain from killing living things.
- Refrain from stealing.
- Refrain from unchastity (sensuality, sexuality, lust).
- Refrain from lying.
- Refrain from taking intoxicants.
- Refrain from taking food at inappropriate times (after noon).
- Refrain from singing, dancing, playing music or attending entertainment programs (performances).
- Refrain from wearing perfume, cosmetics and garland (decorative accessories).
- Refrain from sitting on high chairs and sleeping on luxurious, soft beds.
- Refrain from accepting money.

Our days started early, really early. At first I was a bit angry at why we needed to be woken up at 4am. I was off to a bad start but the first mornings readings/lecture entitled "The Power of 5am" was beautiful and made me feel like maybe I should just trust in the system instead of constantly trying to control things and make them better, which is very American of me.

According to the first morning reading, 5am is the only hour of the day that is truly peaceful. Before that, you still have people up late, drinking and partying.

By 6am you have people waking up rushing to work, stressed and unhappy. But at 5am, nobody is awake and the air just feels peaceful.

Other things I wasn't too happy about included the fact that we weren't allowed to eat anything after noon, which meant we'd have to survive on two vegetarian meals a day. Aside from not speaking, we also weren't allowed to listen to music, watch tv, read books or even write. I ended up breaking the rules a bit a wrote a post card each to my mother and father telling them all the things I've assumed they knew and the things I wanted to get off my chest but never did. It was because of these post cards that my dad after 28 years first told me that he loved me. I always knew that he did, but it was the first time the words ever came out of his mouth and it meant a lot.

One thing I didn't realize how much I'd enjoy was the chores. My duty was raking leaves, but honestly, thinking back, even if I was assigned to clean toilets I would have gotten a lot out of it either way. The chores was more of a duty, and for the first time in my life I did things mindfully. Here is what our daily schedule looked like.

Daily Schedule

04.00 ***   Wake up   *** = Monastery bell
04.30   Morning Reading
04.45   Sitting meditation
05.15   Yoga / Exercise - Mindfulness in motion
07.00 ***   Dhamma talk & Sitting meditation
08.00   Breakfast & Chores
10.00 ***   Dhamma talk
11.00   Walking or standing meditation
11.45 ***   Sitting meditation
12.30   Lunch & chores
14.30 ***   Meditation instruction & Sitting meditation
15.30   Walking or standing meditation
16.15 ***   Sitting meditation
17.00 ***   Chanting & Loving Kindness meditation
18.00   Tea & hot springs
19.30 ***   Sitting meditation
20.00   Group walking meditation
20.30 ***   Sitting meditation
21.00 ***   Bedtime
(the gates will be closed at 21.15)
21.30 ***   LIGHTS OUT

It took me ten days of 'not thinking' to figure these things out. I am greatly honored to be able to share my experience with all of my friends and loved ones. Please read the following mindfully, as they were life changing revelations I discovered.

Johnny FD

1. **Being alone isn't the same as loneliness.**
If you can't eat alone in a public restaurant, or find yourself reaching for your cell phone or something to do anytime you're waiting and standing or sitting alone, you were just like me and everyone else in society. We always have to look busy, or be doing something, or with someone. Why? Can't we just be?

2. **There are Two types of Happiness** - and most of us only know the first.
The first type of happiness is through stimulation - Doing something, eating something, buying something or having something that makes us happy. Some external factor, whether it is music, a friend, or something is the source of our smiles. Whether it talking to someone, listening to your favorite song, eating food food, or even hanging out with friends. These aren't bad things, but it makes us depenant.

The second type of happiness is just being. It took me 13 days to finally just be able to sit, alone, at a restaurant, doing nothing, thinking about nothing, looking forward to nothing, just to be able to smile and realize that I'm happy, just because.

3. **Our possessions posses Us -**
Before moving to Koh Tao, I was in a car dealership trying to figure out a monthly payment to buy a new Corvette. If I had been able to afford it, I would have been stuck paying $800 a month for the next four years, and would never have been able to travel.

The $800 Louis Vuitton Handbag is the same price as a round trip plane ticket and a few days of expenses in Paris. yet, I know 20 girls with LV bags, and only 1 that has ever been.

4. **The Duty of Effort is today, and even tomorrow we may die -**
Whatever our Duty, Job, or Chore is to do, instead of trying to rush through it to empty our inbox, we should realize that our inbox will never be empty, even when we die. So we might as well enjoy the act of working by doing it mindfully and live in the moment, enjoying every minute of it.

5. **We are fine exactly the way we are -**
Whoever we are, is okay. if we can't even love ourselves, how can we expect others to love us?

6. **When we get angry at someone, or something, it hurts us more than it hurts them.**
It's funny that we can relive angry moments that happened years in the past so easily. We can bring them up in our minds and feel hatred and anger as if it was happening to us today. Friends may come and go, but enemy's accumulate. By being mad at someone, does it hurt us more than it hurts them? The answer is definitely yes, so why do that to ourselves? We need to just let go and let karma take over.

7. **Material things can never make us happy as they are fleeting -**

Every time I buy something, before I buy it, in the days, hours or months I dream about it, I smile. But soon after I have it, the smile disappears and I want something else. Expensive things cause more stress in life, and we really don't need it.

When I drove a Porsche, I always had to put the top up so people wouldn't fuck with it. Everyone I met assumed I was a pompous, spoiled asshole. People expected and treated me differently, and not in a good way. The only thing to do to make myself feel better was think of them as jealous, or envious, but that never made me happy. Everyone would ask why I didn't buy the 911 Turbo instead. No one was ever happy for me to have acquired my dream car, and my dream turned out not to be what I expected. When I drove my Celica, Miata, or even my 87' Nissan, I was happy and no one ever treated me with ill will.
So why do we think luxurious things, expensive things can make us happy? Is it because we want to fit in, or is it because we want to have what others have? Either way, I finally realized that I don't need it.

There is actually very little we need in life, and the most basic things are, the happier and more free we become.

My final thoughts:
If you agreed with any of the above or learned anything from it, please do yourself a favor and realize that the worst thing we could do is simply read it, nod our heads and then never think about it again. Even worse is reading it and saying to yourself, oh I already know this.
It took me 10 days of living it, to realize it for myself and have it really settle in and will try to do my best everyday for the rest of my life to remember these things I've learned and actually live them

Airfare: How I got my job to pay for my airfare to Thailand

Johnny FD

This won't work for everyone, but who knows, you might as well give it a shot. A lot of guys quit their jobs before coming out here to Thailand. Don't. Whatever money you saved up is good, but trust me, if you come out here with enough savings for 3 months, there is a good chance you'll wish you could stay for 6. Personally, I made a deal with the company I worked for that I would work remotely part time, take a huge pay cut and come back every three months to work during the busy events in exchange for them letting me expense my airfare to and from Thailand. For what ever reason, including tax write offs but also just because it sounds better, companies are more willing to let you run up high travel expenses than to just give you more money. So whatever your job, even if you're a plumber, instead of quitting your job, figure out when a really busy time of the year is and promise to come back and work for those few months.

If your work is something that can be done online and remotely, even better. I have a friend that randomly decided the wanted to live in Manhattan, in the heart of New York City. The IT company he works for is in Silicon Valley, Northern California, the exact opposite side of the country. They don't have an office in New York and have no reason to be there, but instead of quitting his job, he simply asked if he could work remotely and fly in once a month for meetings. Surprising the company agreed and even pay for his internet, and subsidize part of his rent since he's not using office space. They pay for him to fly into San Francisco once a month and put him in a hotel for a few days so he can show his face and still be part of the team, but other than that, he does Skype meetings and works through email.

Whatever your job is, figure out if there's any possible way you can keep it and still go to Thailand for 3 months. If you can't, find a way to get fired. Seriously. If you quit your job, you get nothing. But if you get fired, you can collect unemployment insurance and use it to fund your life and travels. You'll have to have the paperwork sent to a friend or family member and pretend you are still in the country actively seeking work, but it can be done. I know it sounds immoral and I expect a lot of people, to think it's wrong, but it's up to you. At the end of the day, that money was from all the taxes you've paid over the years, but I completely understand if it's not something you are comfortable doing. A third way to get your airfare paid for, is if your income is high enough and you have your own business, expense it and write it off during tax season. Just have a meeting while you're here in Thailand and call it a business trip.

Tattoos: Where to get authentic bamboo style Thai tattoos done by a monk, for free.

Getting tattoos in Thailand is part of the experience and before I came, I had virgin skin and now am pretty much covered. Just make sure you are ready for the commitment as getting one tattoo always leads to getting three more. There is a temple about an hour away from Bangkok called Wat Bang Phra, I found a taxi driver that spoke decent English and arranged for him to pick me up early the next morning so I could get there at 8am. I don't remember exactly what I paid, but it was less than 2,000 baht ($66US) and he drove me there, translated for me, waited around for a few hours while I got my tattoo, took me to dinner, then drove me back home. The tattoo itself is free, but you are require to buy cigarettes and flowers as a donation for upkeep of the temple for 70 baht ($2US). I know it's a bit random to buy cigarettes for a monk, but this is Thailand. The Monks only tattoo men but as a female you get a tattoo with clear oil that disappears after a few days and still get the blessing and protection.

You start off by choosing a tattoo from a big binder, most people are encouraged to get the standard one on their upper back for protection and good luck as their first. I chose to get two that day as it was quite a far trip, and it turns out that's all I could handle anyways. It was painful, and I mean, really painful. Imagine getting stabbed by a pin 6,000 times and never getting used to the pain. The tattoos are done with traditional bamboo sticks and a homemade ink that's a mixture of palm oil, Chinese ink and possibility snake venom. The needles are reused and sanitized only by dipping them into some alcohol for a second. In retrospect it wasn't the most sanitary, the only good news is there's never been a report of someone getting HIV in Thailand from bamboo needles since there is no reservoir like normal tattoo needles have.

After the tattoo the head monk sits you down, preforms a sacred kata that is supposed to seal in the magic and protection of your new tattoo. It was honestly, a really spiritual experience for me even though it wasn't my intention. I ended up donating an additional 1,000 baht to the monastery The monk also gave me a list of rules to keep, mainly not going around thinking I'm now invincible because of my protection tattoos, but also a random one about not spitting into a toilet, something I haven't done since, just in case.

If you're thinking about getting a tattoo in Thailand, I would only recommend going to the temple if you want the monastery experience. Even though the tattoo was technically free, by the time you add up the donations and taxi fare, I could have just paid for the same tattoo somewhere else. If you're in Koh Tao I would highly recommend getting a tattoo done by Bu at Siam Tattoo which is up the hill from the Muay Thai gym. Bu does the best bamboo tattoos in Thailand and is one of the few people in the world that can do shading with it. Phuket also has some really good tattoo shops, Golden Needle is very well known for quality full color pieces and sleeves but there are many other good ones as well. Prices are about 50% - 75% less than what you would pay back home. Be careful when negotiating prices however, as it's not worth saving a few dollars and getting sub par or rushed work. Instead ask what they charge for an hourly rate and base your financial decision off of that instead.

Exchanging Cash vs. Travelers Checks: Why neither are a great idea.
A lot of people come to Thailand with traveler's checks and end up having a hard time cashing them. They also get high fees when they do finally cash them in. Others bring cash, which is a mistake I did the first time I came as well. When I first made the move to Thailand I brought most of my savings in cash, which was about $3,000US at the time, thinking it would be the best thing to do. Turns out, it was a nightmare. First, I was ultra paranoid carrying around my life savings with me during the first two days it takes to get from the airport to where I was actually going to be staying in Koh Tao.

I was afraid to keep my money in my hotel room so carried it on me at all times which was a bit scary as well. I tried to get a Thai bank account but they wanted a lot of paperwork that I couldn't provide as a tourist. I ended up stashing the money in a locker at some shop which in retrospect wasn't the best idea either. Eventually I convinced a Thai person to help me open an account and I deposited the money, but it wasn't worth the hassle. In Thailand unless you have crisp, brand new $100US bills some places won't even take the money, and if you have smaller notes, they actually give you less value for them. For the past two years I've only carried $200US cash for just in case emergencies and the rest of my money I withdraw through ATM.

Withdrawing from an ATM: How to get all of your ATM Fees refunded.
The best way to get money in Thailand is though the ATM which takes pretty much all ATM cards from around the world without any hassle. There are ATMs everywhere, literally you will never have to spend more than a few minutes or walk more than a block to find one in most towns. The conversion rates are virtually identical to the exchange rates you get for cash, so aside from the 150 baht ($5US) fee there is no reason not to use ATMs for everything.

There are two ways to avoid paying a lot in ATM fees. The first, and the easiest, is simply to withdraw your maximum limit each time which is 10,000 baht ($333US) and sometimes up to 15,000 baht ($500US), that way you are only withdrawing money two times a month on average so your monthly fees will only be around 300 baht ($10US) which isn't too bad. I time my withdraws to pay for my rent and my gym fees at the same time so I never have too much cash on me. But for most places, especially if you use your own lock and hide your cash, having a few thousand baht in your room isn't that big of a deal, just don't have bar girls over.

The second way to find a bank that refunds your ATM Fees. I use Charles Schwab which is a U.S. based investment bank that automatically refunds all atm fees, no matter what. Instead of my bank charging me $3 to withdraw from a non-bank atm and the other bank charging me another $5, I get zero fees and still a really good exchange rate. Best of all the bank account was absolutely free to open and I did it online. To open an account you first need to open a free brokerage account, which is what you would use if you wanted to trade stocks. With that, you can open a free high yield investors checking account. None of them have any fees or minimum balances, making it the perfect bank. The only catch is if you are traveling for more than 6 months they may close your account, the trick would be to make a U.S. based purchase online with that card before your six months are up, or maybe use it for five and switch to another atm card for the rest of your trip.

Fidelity Cash Management Account also refunds you all atm fees just like Schwab without any fees. There are a total of 49 banks in the US that refund ATM fees so do your research as some of them come with direct deposit requirements and minimum balances, but Schwab is the one I personally use as their customer service is excellent.

If you like in the U.K. look into Caxton FX, they won't refund you the 150 baht the Thai bank charges you, but at least they won't charge you a fee themselves. If you live somewhere else in the world, do a quick google search in your own language or country and see what comes up, or you can try to open a US based account if possible.

Whatever you do, make sure you have at least two separate ATM cards, as this will be your main way of withdrawing money and it's very easy to misplace or lose one. I personally have three ATM cards just in case and have all of my online banking linked to each other so I can easily move money from one account to another.

Johnny FD

Credit Cards: How to avoid the unsuspecting 3% international currency exchange fee.

Most people don't think about it, but almost all credit card companies charge a 2%-3% international currency exchange fee for purchases in a different currency. The worst thing about it is they often don't bill you for it for 30 days afterward so you get hit with all of them at once out of no where.

Luckily, if you do your research, you'll find credit cards with no foreign transaction fees. I personally use the Capital One Venture One card, which has zero foreign fees and no annual fee, making it the perfect travel card. You won't use your credit card too often in Thailand as most places take cash, but it's perfect for booking flights and hotels while in Asia. Often for visa runs I'll book a cheap flight and check out a neighboring country for a few days. I've made short trips to Kuala Lumpuar in Malaysia, Singapore to watch a MMA fight, Bali to spend New Years eve and the Philippines to go trekking in the rice fields. Often you can get return airfare through budget airlines such as Air Asia for less than $120US if you book ahead of time. By using a credit card with no foreign transaction fees, you'll save $5-$10 each time you book a hotel or flight while in Asia. I've also used my credit card to book an international return flight from Thailand to the US and back to Thailand for close to $1,500 US which would have costed me an additional $45US if I had used another credit card.

If you live outside of the US do a quick google search for what credit cards in your country don't charge foreign transaction fees. Again, it's a good idea to have at least two or even three credit cards while traveling as you can either lose one or easily get locked out of one while traveling. I always call my credit card companies ahead of time before I leave home to tell them I'll be traveling for three months. Often they'll make a note your account but it's not a perfect system as there is a 50% chance they'll still lock you out, so make sure you have a backup or two.

Bringing your Muay Thai and MMA gear with you:
Although it's very tempting to come to Thailand to buy a set of authentic Thai gear, it's often much cheaper to get at home if you can find it on sale. I bought a bunch of gear on titlemma.com when they had a sale and it ended up being a lot cheaper than getting gear in Thailand.

TRIUMPH UNITED THAI TRUNKS LARGE BLACK
 Color: BLACK Size: LARGE Price: $8.99
I paid 270 baht, and the cheapest quality muay thai shorts you can find in Thailand will be around 700 baht.

TRIUMPH UNITED PRO SHIN/INSTEP GUARDS
 Color: BLACK Size: LARGE Price: $13.49
I paid 400 baht, and they would have been closer to 1,200 baht here in Thailand for something of similar quality.

Triumph United HEATSEEKER 2 TRAINING GLOVES VELCRO 12 OZ BLACK
Size: 12 OZ Price: $13.49
I paid 400 baht and they would have been 1,600 baht here in Thailand.

Johnny FD

THROWDOWN MEXICAN STYLE HANDWRAPS
Price: $1.79
I paid 55 baht for these and they would have been 300 here in Thailand, however, these I regret buying as the quality wasn't good.

All my gear, still holding up nicely after 2 months of hard daily use.

Overall, I'm really impressed with the quality of the Triumph United gear. The only thing that wore off is the label that says 12oz which at least the rest of the gear is still perfect. Supposedly Triumph gear is modeled after the legendary Winning gear that is extremely expensive and high end. Either way, I really like my TU gloves and they are perfect for pads and bagwork.
The other nice thing about having non thai-brands is you never get your gear mixed up with other people at the gyms. Since there are really only four brands everyone uses in Thailand, everyone's gear looks exactly the same. My shorts are also a big hit with the Thai trainers as they say something in Thai that isn't common. No idea what actually says though. Hopefully it's not something stupid.

How to Speak Restaurant Thai: The ten or so words I use on a daily basis. I've been living in Thailand off and on for the last few years now and still can't speak Thai, mainly because I never needed to. In Koh Tao and on most of the islands you never need to speak Thai and if you try to practice it with locals that speak English, they get annoyed. Even in restaurants, most of the workers are actually from Burma and speak better English than they do Thai anyways. In Phuket, everyone spoke English, and it wasn't until I moved up here to Chiang Mai did I really wish I knew it.

Even though I don't actually speak Thai, I've figured out over the years how to communicate and how to get what I want. The first rule is only speak Thai to people that don't speak English. I don't know how guys don't realize how annoying they are being speaking their shit Thai to locals that speak decent English. It's usually old white guys that don't have good social skills in their own language either, so I can see why that happens.

Second, don't dumb down your English to people that speak good English just because they are Asian. If a Thai person speaks semi-fluent English, talk to them like a normal human being and not a three year old. It happens to me all of the time, usually with older white men, even when I tell them I'm American, they continue to talk to me like I'm fucking retarded, stop that, it's annoying as shit. Some basic social awareness goes a long way.

However, if someone truly doesn't speak English, talk to them slowly and don't use any unnecessary words. I respect English people for never dumbing down their language, which is helpful in the long run for locals to learn proper English, but what's funny is they don't realize by using colloquialisms and humor, it's confusing the shit out of the person you're trying to order food from.
So here are the basics.

If you want to order Chicken Pad Thai, don't say:

"Ummm...I'm thinking about having the chicken pad thai, is it quite good here? Actually, yes, definitely I'll have that."

Instead just say, "Chicken Pad Thai", hold up a finger to show the number one and smile. Most people will understand that even if they don't speak English. If you want to order it in Thai, simply say:

"Pad Thai Gai" and use the word "kup" (You can get away with pronouncing it as 'Cup') at the end if you're a guy, or "kaa" at the end if you're a girl to be polite. So basically you would say:

"Pad Thai Gai, Kup."

Obviously, Gai means chicken, which is what you'll be eating 95% of the time so remember how to say it. You can get away with saying "Guy" which sounds close enough.

Kup is actually pronounced Krup, but I'm trying to keep things as simple as possible for everyone to remember so I'll drop certain letters if they don't make a huge difference.

In case you're confused about the who Kup vs. Ka thing, it's easy, don't over think it. If you are male, you will always say krup. If you are a girl, you will always say kaa. It doesn't change if you are talking to a man or a women or about a man or a women.
The second thing you'll want to learn how to say is "Not Spicy" as a lot of people coming to Thailand for the first time will be overwhelmed by chilies.

If you don't want your dish to be spicy at all, say, "Mai Ped"

"Mai" means, no, not, or without. Remember the word "My" as it'll come in handy often.

"Ped" means Spicy, think of "Pet" even though it's slightly different they'll understand you.

So not spicy is basically, "My Pet." or if you want to say it correctly say "Mai Ped" and of course you can add Kup to they end to be polite, saying "Mai Ped Kup"

If you want your food to be a little bit spicy say, "Ped Nit Noi" Phed as you already learned means spicy. "Nit Noi" means a little bit. So say, "Ped Nit Noi Kup" if you want your food to be only a little bit spicy.

To order Chicken Pad Thai without any spiciness as a man you would say: "Pad Thai Gai, Mai Ped, Kup."

To order Chicken Pad Thai with just a little bit of spiciness as a man you would say: "Pad Thai Gai, Ped, Nit Noi, Kup."

Congratulations, you can now order food without burning a hole in your mouth, all while being polite!

Okay so you're going to want to learn to order more than one dish, here are the ones I eat on a daily basis.

Chicken with Fried Basil Leaves: Pad Ka Pow Gai – Pad, the same one used in Pad Thai, means Fried, but in reality means stir fried and Gai is still chicken.

You may also want to order the same dish but with pork instead which is "Moo" think of a the sound a cow makes, "Moo." No one in Thailand eats Beef very often as it isn't popular and doesn't taste very good. So the easiest way to think of it is pork is your new red meat. Just say, "Moo" every time you are tempted to order beef, which is actually "Nueh" which you don't need to remember because you will literally almost never eat it here.

To order Pork and Basil you would say, "Pad Ka Pow Moo. Kup." Just remember, Pad, and KaPow! The sound a super hero makes in old comic books.

Even though you could technically remember a few dishes by name, in the long run you'll be happy learning what eat of the words mean as the same words often repeat in every dish.

One addition you'll want to make to almost every dish is adding a fried egg on top. Eggs in Thailand are a good cheap source of protein and taste delicious. If you are worried about cholesterol by eating too many whole eggs, you'll be happy to hear that it's a myth, but don't take my word for it, do your own research. Whole eggs are one of the healthiest things you'll eat in Thailand, especially since I'm pretty sure most eggs here are somewhat free range as the yolks are a bright beautiful orange that only comes from eating grass.

Johnny FD

To order a fried egg on top of your meal say, "Kai Dao, Kup." Egg is Kai. If you want two fried eggs, which is an easy and cheap way to get more protein you would say, "Kai Dao, Song. Krup." Song is two, or simply say, "Kai Dao." and hold up two fingers.

You may also want to learn the number one, which is "Nueng" but in the beginning you can get away with using the universal hand signs for numbers. Rice will automatically come with most dishes, but in case they ask if you want rice, it is pronounced "Kao" think of "Cow." In case you are tempted to complicate things by asking for brown rice because you think it's more healthy, don't. Unless they specifically advertise it, they won't have brown rice. I personally stopped eating brown rice as one, it doesn't taste good with Asian food and second, it's not any better for you. Again, do your own research but you can start by googling "Brown Rice Bulletproof."

If you don't want any rice at all, you would say, "Mai Yao Kao." Mai, as we learned before means no. "Ow" means want and "Kao" is rice. So you are literally saying, No want rice.
Now be warned that if you ask for no rice, they'll freak out and get really confused. In Asian culture, food is rice, with a little bit of meat and vegetables as flavor. It's the reason why in Chinese, people don't ask if you've had lunch yet, they ask if you've eaten rice yet. So if you're avoiding rice, you'll need to ask for something else as a substitute because they'll feel embarrassed giving you two spoonfuls of meat and a tiny bit of vegetables. I'll talk about that more in the next chapter of eating paleo.
If you want an extra large portion of food, as the Thai portions may be too small, just say, "P-Set, Kup." Sometimes I'll say, "P-Set, Yai, Kup." P-Set means Special Set, or Large Set. "Yai" means Large. So a big version of fried basil with chicken would be, "Pad KaPow Gai, P-Set, Kup."

One thing you might want to learn how to say is, "Please don't include any random organ meats or chicken blood in my food." I know it sounds strange, and 98% of the time food doesn't come with it anyways, but there are certain dishes where you'll wish you knew this phrase. The most common dish that comes with a side of cubed, gelatine chicken blood is "Kao Man Gai" which is just Chicken Rice. It's one of my favorite dishes in Thailand and actually originally comes from the Hainan Proviance of China. It's basically just chicken and rice, but it's steamed together which gives the rice a really nice chicken flavor. To ask for no chicken blood it's technically, "Mai Sai Luat" but it's easier just to remember, "please no random insides" as a catch all phrase instead of trying to remember how to say kidney, liver and intestine.
So as a catch all, just say, "Mai Ow Sai" and to help illustrate it, point to your stomach with a finger in a circular motion. We've already learned the phrase, "Mai Ow" which means don't want, so just remember "Sai" as in "Insides" and you'll be fine.

Other dishes that use random organ meats are some noodle soups and some curries, especially ones that are premade and you just point to.
What I do is ask, the easy phrase, "Gai, Mai?" and if they said no, I ask "Moo, Mai?" Which means, Chicken? And Pork? If they say don't say yes to either of

those, I most likely don't want to eat it and move on. Technically you are saying, "Chicken, No?" But "No" at the end of the sentence makes it into an easy question.

The dish I eat most often, as it's usually decently big, is healthy, tastes good, and is always a bit different wherever I go so I never get sick of it is literally, Chicken with Mixed Vegetables. Order by saying, "Pad Paak Ruam Gai" Pad is fried. Paak means vegetables. Ruam is mixed. And Gai is chicken. Another easy one I eat often is Stir Fried Chilies and Chicken, which is "Pad Prick Gai." Or if you want it with pork it's "Pad Prick Moo." Prick is chilies. "Pad Prick Moo. Kai Dao. Kup." Means, "May I please have a dish of stir fried chilies with pork and a fried egg on top"

This is "Pad Prick Moo, Kai Dao." (Fried Chilies Pork, Fried Egg)

With that you can ask for different spiciness levels, I'll say, "Ped Ped" which means extra spicy, and you may say, "Ped Nit Noi" which is only a little bit spicy.

"Pad Prick Moo. Kai Dao. Ped Nit Noi. Kup."

Easy? Good. It's supposed to be. The best thing about learning restaurant Thai is that you'll get to practice it a few times everyday, permanently embedding it into your brain. The easiest thing to do is write down some of your favorite dishes on a piece of paper and keep it in your wallet, it's what got me through the first few months and how I continue to learn new dishes.

Basic Polite Thai: There are a few other words that you'll use everyday that would be beneficial to know. First is the standard greeting you'll say to everyone 10x a day. "Sa-wa-dee Kup" think of SWAT (the Police Force) and D-Cups.

How are you is "Sa-Buy-De Kup?" (Sabai Dee Krup) which means, "Feeling good, yes?" So to answer, just repeat the feeling good part without the "yes?" So you would say, "Sabai Dee" to say that you are good. Another easy response is responding, "Sabai, Sabai." Which a most Thai people will get a laugh at because it's something only laid back, island people say, and it basically means, "I'm feeling good, I'm feeling good" or "I'm chilling and relaxing."

The other phrase that you'll learn to use quite often and is a good mindset to have while traveling in Thailand is "Mai Been Rai." (or you can say "Mai Been Lai," as Thai people can't tell the difference between L and R for whatever reason. It means, never mind, no worries. I use this a lot when they are out of something, or I try to make a special request that they don't understand. Eventually you'll want to learn how to count from 1 to 999. In the mean time, the easiest way is to hold up fingers for anything between 1-10 and when you buy stuff and don't know what it costs, just hand them a 100 baht note and see if you get back any change. Before I learned the number system in Thai, I would just guess how much something would cost, and then hand them a note that was slightly larger. If you're eating Thai food, it'll almost always be less than 100 baht, so just say "Check Please" hand it to them and the note and watch their facial expressions and actions for confirmation. If they give you a look like, "what the fuck is this, that's not enough." then hand them another 100 baht note. If they start digging up change, then just stand there like you expected it in the first place.

Doing this little trick, I've never been over charged by much but if you really want to get the best deals you have to learn the basic numbers in Thai.
A trick to always having small bills is every time you withdraw money from the ATM, instead of withdrawing a solid number such as 10,000 baht, take instead 9,900 baht. The machine will dispense smaller bills. Also, every time you go into a 711 break your 1,000 baht notes, they are Thailand's money changer.
Realize it's both rude and a pain in the ass to try to break a 1,000 baht note in a local Thai shop, especially if your meal is under 100 baht. Also realize that a lot of Taxi drivers won't have change to break your big notes either, so always carry plenty of 100 baht notes.

To ask for the check properly in Thai, you would say, "Check Bin Kup." And if you want to ask how much something costs you would say, "Thaew Roy Kup" but be prepared to get an answer in Thai if you do. You might be better off just asking, "How much?" in the meantime until you learn the numbers.
In the first edition of this book I included a chapter teaching you how to count from 1-1,000 but I decided to take it out and put it on my blog instead as everyone was skipping that chapter anyways. You won't need to know how to count until you've actually been in Thailand for a while so look for it on my blog when you're ready.

Special Diets in Thailand: Vegetarian, Vegan, Religious and Paleo

It's possible to have a special diet in Thailand but remember that you're a guest in another culture and you need to be open minded and tolerant of theirs firstly. It's funny that after being in Thailand for just 3 months, I would say, "I lived in Thailand." I honestly believed I was like a citizen and had rights. Now after being here off and on for the past four yeas, I've realized that I'm a visitor and always will be and I need to respect that.

Not eating pork or being Vegetarian in Thailand is relatively easy especially if you eat eggs. If you don't eat pork for whatever reason, just learn to order "Gai" which is chicken, and if something is pre-made, just ask, "Gai, Mai?" You can also learn to say, "Mai Ow, Moo" which is "No Want Pork."

The easiest way, no matter what your special requests are is to have someone write it down for you in Thai and show it every time you order food. Have them write down specifically what you can and cannot yet. If you do it verbally, there is a big chance you'll get something you didn't expect, but honestly, you just have to learn to be flexible. The other option is to do all of your own cooking. There are plenty of supermarkets in Thailand and you can buy a stove top and gas cooking set for less than 1,000 baht ($33US) Cooking yourself will be the only 100% sure way you'll get what you expect all of the time.

If you choose to eat out at restaurants, realize that even I get something random that I didn't expect at least once every two weeks while I'm here. I usually just try a tiny bit of it and eventually end up eating around it. Not many people know this about me but I was strict vegetarian for six months. Even after I stopped, during my time at Phuket Top Team I would eat vegetarian for breakfast and lunch everyday along with, now Ilya Grad who was training there at the time and recently just won the WMC I-1 Championship at 72kg. We didn't plan it, but after eating vegetarian food everyday, we noticed that we wouldn't be tired, sluggish or need a nap, which gave us more energy to train in the afternoons. I don't know if he still does it or not as I haven't talked to him in a while, but it worked.

There are a lot of benefits of being vegetarian and I respect people that are, as they are usually good people that care about animals and the environment However, keeping an open mind and doing more research made me realize that life and food is all about balance. The reason why I stopped eating meat in the first place was after I found out how cruel factory farms treat animals. I continued to not eat meat for health benefits. But I now know that the truth is, being vegetarian is healthier than the standard western diet, but it's not as healthy as eating a sustainable paleo diet. As a vegetarian, you end up eating a lot of pasta, bread, french fries and other things that are terrible for your health and actually not very good for the environment either.

I've stopped eating wheat completely, including bread and pasta, and avoid deep fried foods. I'm not here to try to change anyone's diet or views, but I do encourage everyone to do their own research and stay open mined. I honestly believe that the perfect diet for your health and also the environment as a whole would be a Paleo diet where 80% of your diet is fresh organic non-monsanto gmo vegetables, and the other 20% is healthy fat and protein from coconut oil, butter from grass fed cows, whole eggs from happy free ranged chickens, and meat from grass fed animals, and a bit of sweet potatoes for healthy carbs. The underlying problem isn't eating meat or not. It comes down to money and greed from trying to produce the cheapest meat possible. If everyone stopped eating wheat, sugar, only ate grass fed beef, and truly free range eggs, we would all be healthier, animals would be treated well and there wouldn't be this problem.

If you are a vegan or vegetarian and really want to make a huge difference, lobby your politicians to make all prisons 100% vegetarian. I'm sure people would riot in the beginning, but it'll also make people never want to go back to prison again. 2,019,234 or so people in the U.S. will be forced to stop eating meat, saving the country money and reducing the about of animals slaughtered each year by tons. It'll literally do 2 million times more benefit than you personally not eating meat. Also if you are a vegan or vegetarian for health reasons and you smoke, drink alcohol or eat french fries, you are really being hypocritical.

Personally I came to Thailand trying to eat healthy but realized that there needs to be a balance. I don't drink alcohol, juice, soda or anything with sugar. I don't eat pizza, pasta or bread. I tried asking Thai restaurants to cook my food with butter instead of vegetable oil, and even went as far as bringing a tub of grass-fed gee, which is clarified butter, to have them cook with. But when it comes down to it, the traditional Thai diet is actually pretty healthy and if you look at most Thai people, they aren't fat unless they eat a lot of western food. The reason why I stopped requesting my food to be cooked in butter is first it's kind of a pain in the ass, and second, it makes the Thai food taste funny. I thought about using coconut oil instead but it would still give the food a unique taste. Plus you have to carry it around with you all the time.

I carry about this piece of paper in my wallet that I asked Chon my trainer at the gym to write for me. It basically says, "Please use less oil in my food, and also please don't add any sugar."

Now my modified Asian Paleo diet consists of bulletproof coffee for breakfast, which you can google but it's basically coffee or green tea, grass fed unsalted butter, (you can get Anchor brand in Thailand) and MCT Oil/Coconut Oil all blended together. Sometimes when I get sick of drinking it, I have a glass of coconut milk instead, that I mix with cold water and ice.

For lunch and dinner, I have a standard plate of Thai food with a fried egg or two. Usually it is chicken or pork with mixed vegetables and rice. I made sure to have 2 fish oil tablets afterward to balance out the omega 6 fats in the vegetable oil that all Thai restaurants use. Another more Paleo friendly lunch I would have is buying ½ a roast chicken from the Chicken stands you often see parked in front of 711s and Supermarkets. I'll go into the market to buy a bunch of raw vegetables. For lunch I would have ¼ to ½ a roast chicken with the veggies.

Johnny FD

When I have access to a kitchen I simply scramble 4whole eggs with onions or chives in grass-fed Anchor butter and salt and have that for breakfast or lunch. For dinner you can go to Thai BBQ restaurants where they have a steaming pot of water with a small grill on top usually for 129-200 baht ($4.30 - $6.66US) all you can eat. The Japanese style ones in the mall cost 330 baht ($11US) and are Shabu-Shabu style only which is where you boil the meat in broth kind of like fondue. Recently I discovered non-all you can eat versions that have veggies for 10 baht (33cents) and most meat items for 19 baht. My bill normally comes out to around 120 baht ($4US) per person, slightly less than the buffet. The service, and food quality is higher. Plus you don't end up over eating. At the above restaurants you can have just grilled meat and boiled vegetables making it extremely paleo friendly as long as you don't use the dipping sauces which contain tons of sugar.

Random snacks include Coconut milk and raw almonds for healthy fats. As a treat I eat a few squares of dark chocolate and once in a while I have some fruit, often cut up in coconut milk. A great easy recipe for a delicious healthy dessert is my mango coconut milk tapioca. Basically you just reconstitute some chia seeds into a tapioca like gel, and add cold coconut milk and chilled fruit to it in a bowl. That's really it, I usually use cut up mango, dragon fruit or banana. It tastes like a bad for you dessert but in actuality is better for you than just eating the fruit straight.

My modified Asian Paleo diet isn't perfect, but it's cheap, simple, doesn't confuse Thai people, and it's healthy. I've lost 5kg (11lbs) of fat on this diet so far while keeping all my muscle. It tastes great, I have plenty of energy to train hard, and best of all, it's something that I can get anywhere in Thailand, at any restaurant. Plus it's so easy to follow that it's something that I can see myself doing for as long as I'm here. When it comes down to it, unless you are willing to cook at home, you need to be flexible and open minded.

*Update: In the past 2 months after starting CrossFit here in Chiang Mai I've decided not to compromise and started cooking all of my own food. I moved into an apartment that has a fridge and a bar area with a kitchen sink and set up a 400 baht ($13.34US) stove top. My diet has been eggs, fresh vegetables and meat all cooked in Anchor Grass-Fed Butter. When I feel like I need more energy, I add in sweet potatoes but in general have been totally carb free. Twice a week I will go out to eat BBQ at night with friends and have just grilled meat and vegetables while I'm there.

With this strict paleo diet I'm feeling even better and have lost a ton of weight and fat around my midsection. Here is a photo of my shopping which includes Anchor Brand Grass Fed Butter, Coconut Milk, Eggs, Beef, Pork, Chicken, Veggies, Pink Himalayan Sea Salt, Sunflower Seeds, Raw Almonds and Extra Virgin Olive Oil for Salads.

My biggest fears, and my quest for freedom: Making the plunge into your own 12 weeks in Thailand.

When I first came to Thailand, my biggest fear was leaving the comforts, safety and job security of the United States. Now when I hear my friends talk about taking a 5 day vacation to Panama I ask them, why don't you just go for a few weeks or even a month since you're flying all the way down there anyways? Their response,

"Dude, I can't just leave work for a week, five days is plenty of time."

My fear of losing job security in my career has now been replaced by my fear of working all the time and not having the freedom to travel or follow my passions.

My true biggest fear for a long time has been waking up one day in my mid thirties, being single, with no savings, no house, no career, and still not married. I was afraid that all of my friends would move on without me, get married, buy houses, do well in their careers and I would never be able to catch up.
Now it's happening. I am 31 years old, turning 32 in less than 6 months, my friends are getting married and a lot of them have bought their first homes. Every time I go back to visit, one of my friends has a kid. It's happening, and part of me knows that I want that one day just as bad as they do. I want to get married, have kids, buy my own home and have a solid career with enough money to spend on my family.

However, I wouldn't trade what I have right now, which is basically nothing more than a backpack full of clothes and my freedom for what they have. Financially, it took me a long time to realize this but even though all my friends at home have nice cars, high paying jobs, the newest iPhone and all that, they also have tons of debt. They have credit card bills, a contract for their smart phone, car payments, student loans, and a 30 year mortgage. I have none of that, I have zero debt, no balances, and I used the money I got from selling my car to pay off my student loans. It was tempting to keep that money to travel with, for emergencies, or to buy another car when I moved back, but it was one of the best decisions I ever made.

If my bank account never got down to my last $500 dollars, which I'm scraping by on now, I wouldn't have had the urgency to sit down and finish this book. I never would have focused so hard on training and fighting. It's the sense of urgency you get when someone lights a fire under your ass, it's the uncomfortable situations that bring out the best in you.

My biggest fear now is waking up one day, married to a girl that I'm not passionately in love with, one that I hardly ever even have sex with anymore, with a 30 year mortgage on a house filled with material things that I don't really need, children that I would do anything for and have to because I hate my job and cannot afford to quit. Out of everyone I know that's now married, has kids, a house, I don't think any of them are truly happy. I know they love their kids, but I can also see the fire dying in their eyes. Their only source of excitement is some random hobby they think is their life, and asking me about my adventures.

They even encourage their friends to get married as well, but mainly because they want company in their misery.

Still, knowing all that, knowing how much I will have to sacrifice, how I will willingly enslave myself in order to give my future children the world. Knowing how little they'll actually appreciate it, I still want to get married, have kids and buy a house someday. But when I do, it'll be on my terms and on my time. It will be to a woman that I truly love, one that I would have literally, traveled the entire world to meet, but who knows, she might be waiting for me back in the U.S, in some small town somewhere. Either way, these next few years that I get to travel the world, live in Thailand and focus on nothing but what I am madly passionate about, these memories, these experiences, no one will ever be able to take away from me.

I sincerely hope you get to make the same journey. Whatever you do, make sure it's on your terms. The world is truly like a book, and if you've never traveled, it's like reading only a single chapter. '

Johnny FD

Contact me: How to ask me anything your inquiring mind may want to know. The best way to contact me would be through facebook or on my blog. If you have a question regarding Thailand, Muay Thai, or Training please ask it on the facebook wall or as a comment on the wall so other people can chime in and also benefit from the answer. You'll be surprised how many of the same questions I get over and over again. If the question you ask is covered in the book, don't be surprised if I reference it back to you with a page number or chapter to review. If it's a personal question or something you want to keep private, feel free to send me a private message on facebook.

Also if you enjoyed this book, please do me a huge favor and write a positive, five star review on Amazon. I'll be extremely grateful for it and it'll really help other people decide to buy the book and start their own journey, even if it's just an idea to start traveling more. I honestly think that the more people that read this book, the more likely they will plan their trip sooner than later and start enjoying their lives and following their passions. My goal is to have 50 reviews on amazon for this book, and you can make a huge difference by helping. By you spending two minutes to write one, it'll not only help me but also other people just like you that dream about taking a long vacation away from all the stress of home.

I sincerely hope that this book as inspired you to follow your passions like I have, or at least take the first step to find or what those are, what ever they end up being. Don't wait for time and money to be perfect, the perfect time to go after what you want is right now.

www.MyFightCamp.com The Muay Thai Blog

www.johnnyfd.com - My Lifestyle and Online business blog

www.facebook.com/12weeksinThailand – Like the page and keep in touch.

Warm Regards,

Johnny F.D.

P.S. Help spread the word by making a status on facebook or twitter saying you just finished reading "12 weeks in Thailand: The Good Life on the Cheap" it really helps spread the word.

If you got a lot out of reading this book, or simply enjoyed it, please take a few minutes and write a review either on my facebook wall and/or on Amazon. My goal is to get fifty reviews on Amazon, your review really does help.

Printed in Great Britain
by Amazon.co.uk, Ltd.,
Marston Gate.